TATTOO COLORING BOOK

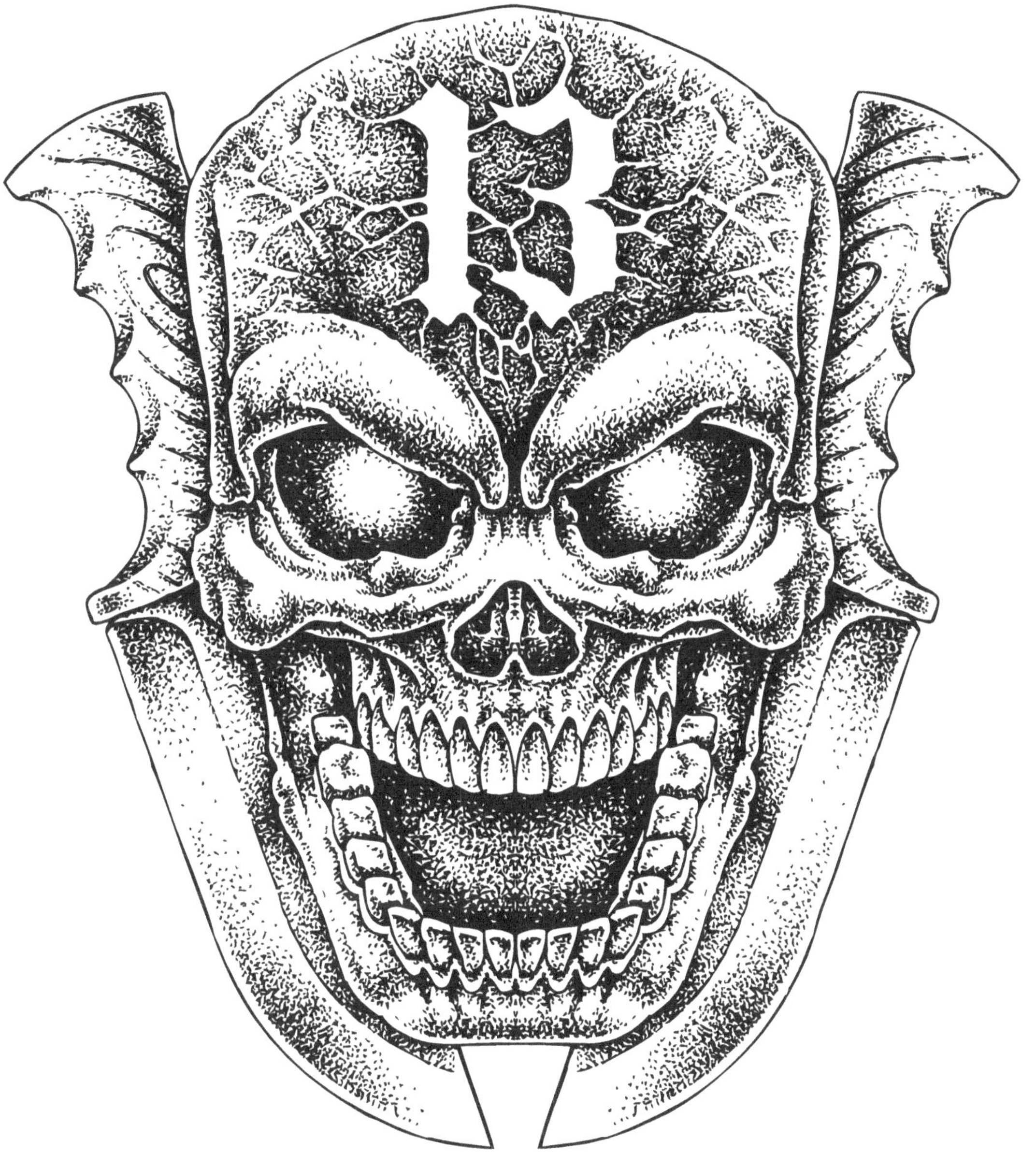

– RUSS FOCUS –

ISBN-13: 978-1727273861 ISBN-10: 1727273869
PUBLISHED BY RUSS FOCUS

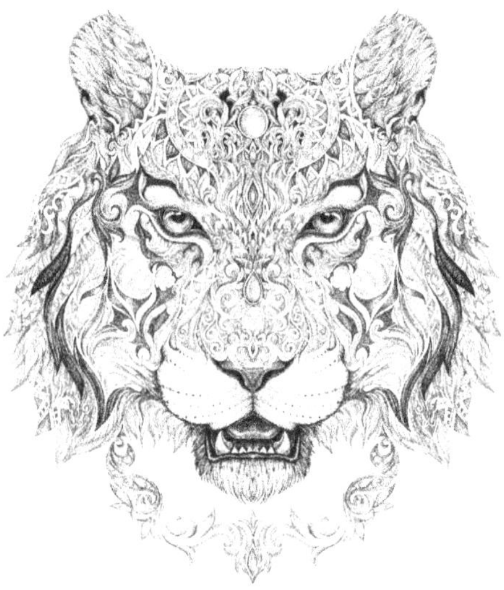
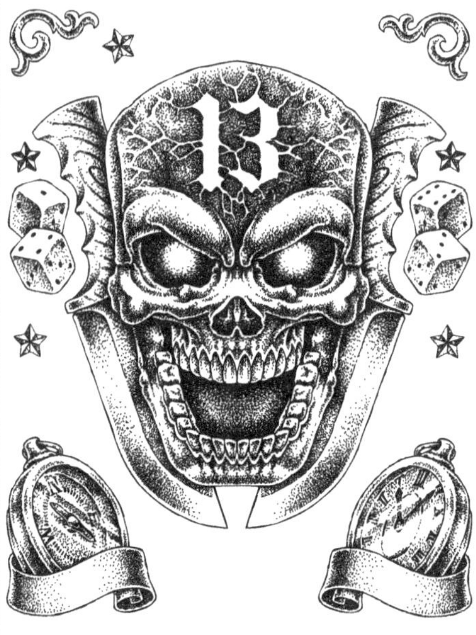
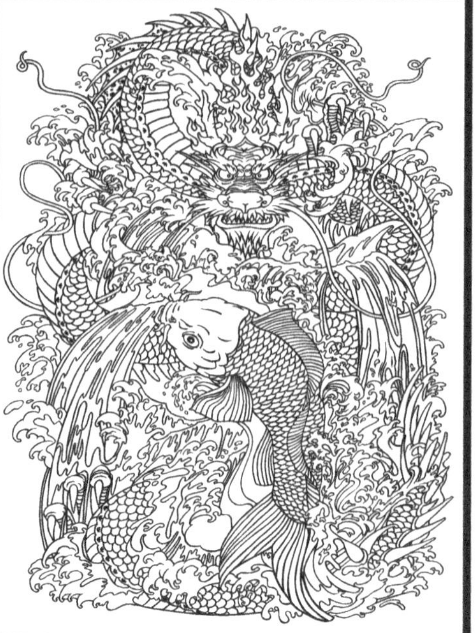
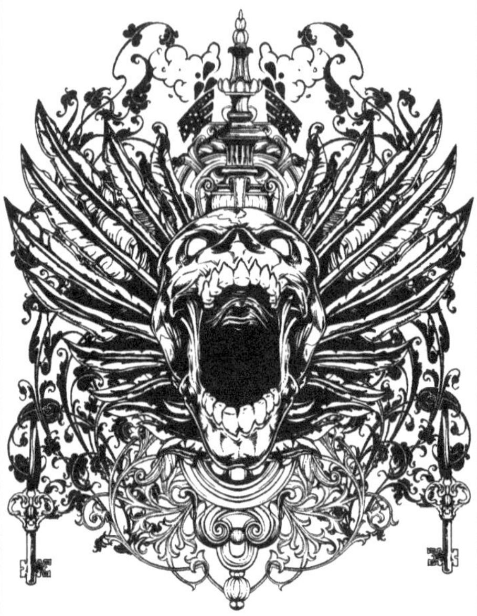

SAMPLE
TATTOO
COLORING
17 of 40
PAGES

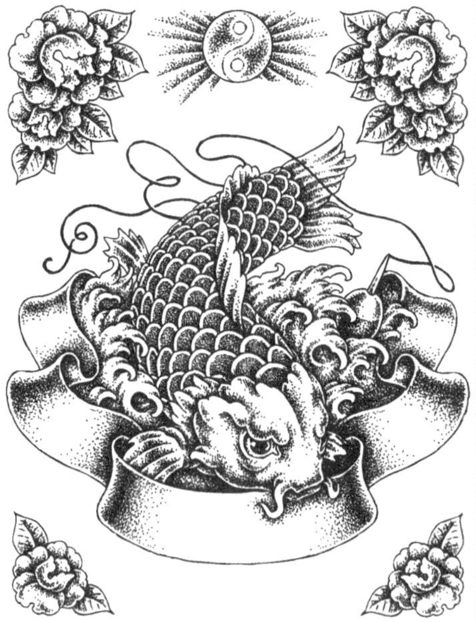
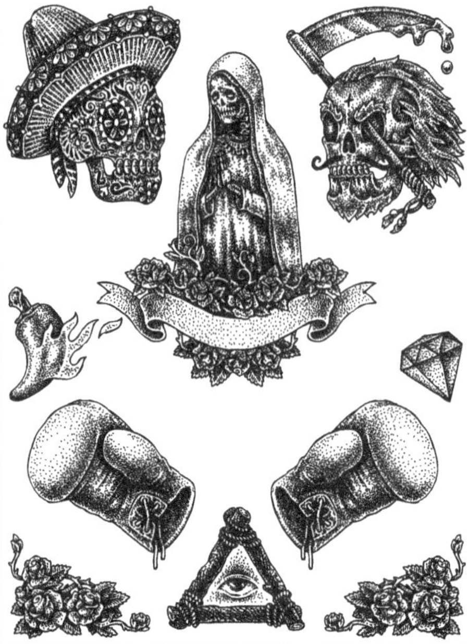
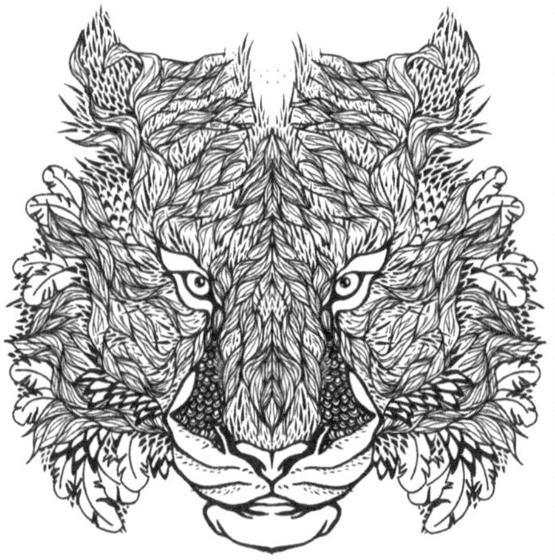
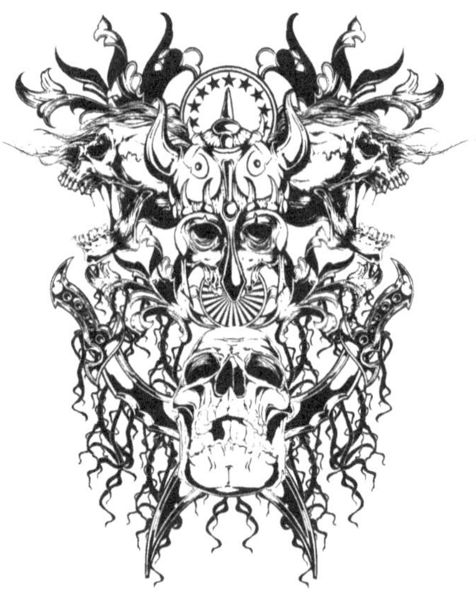

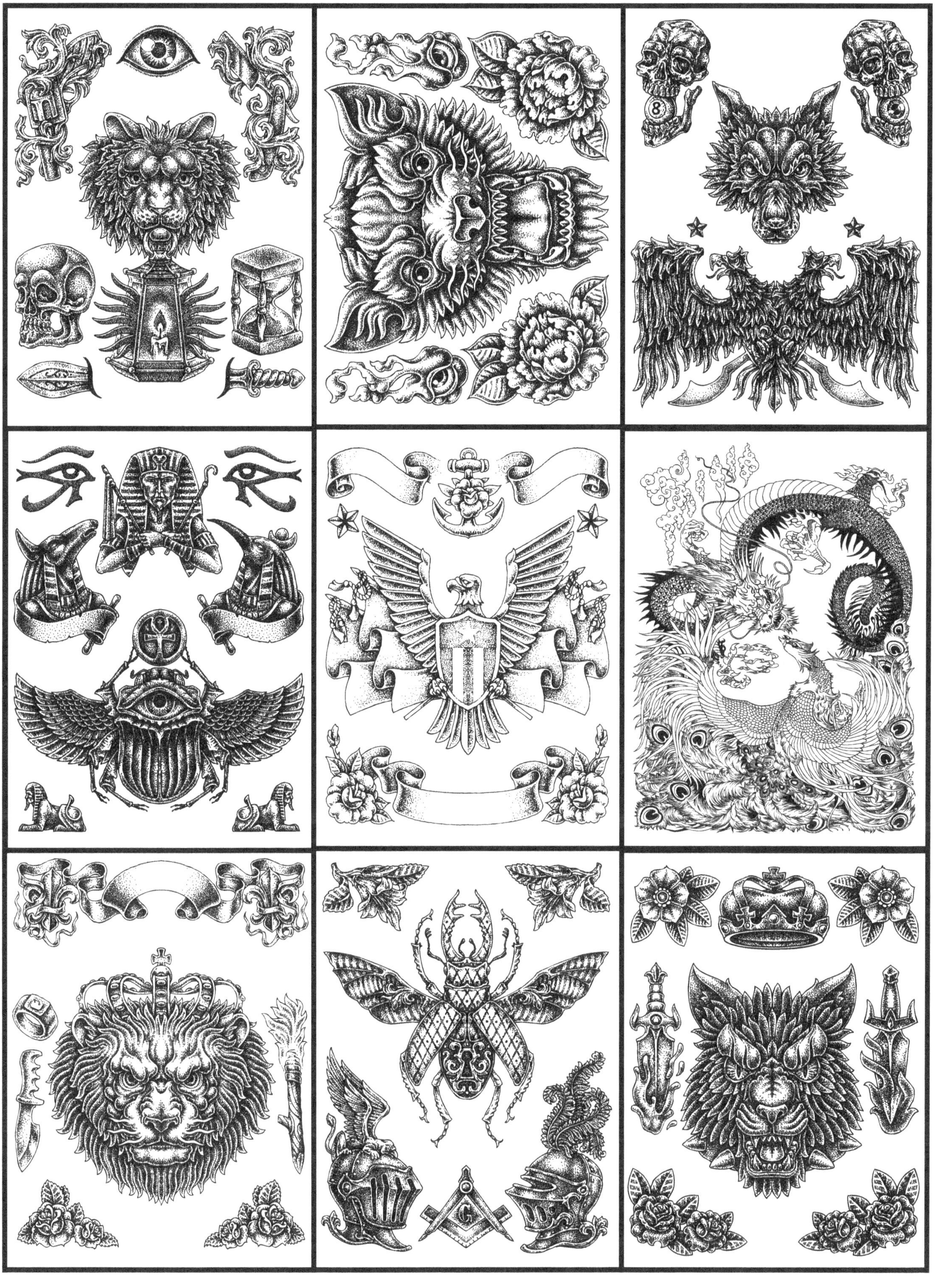

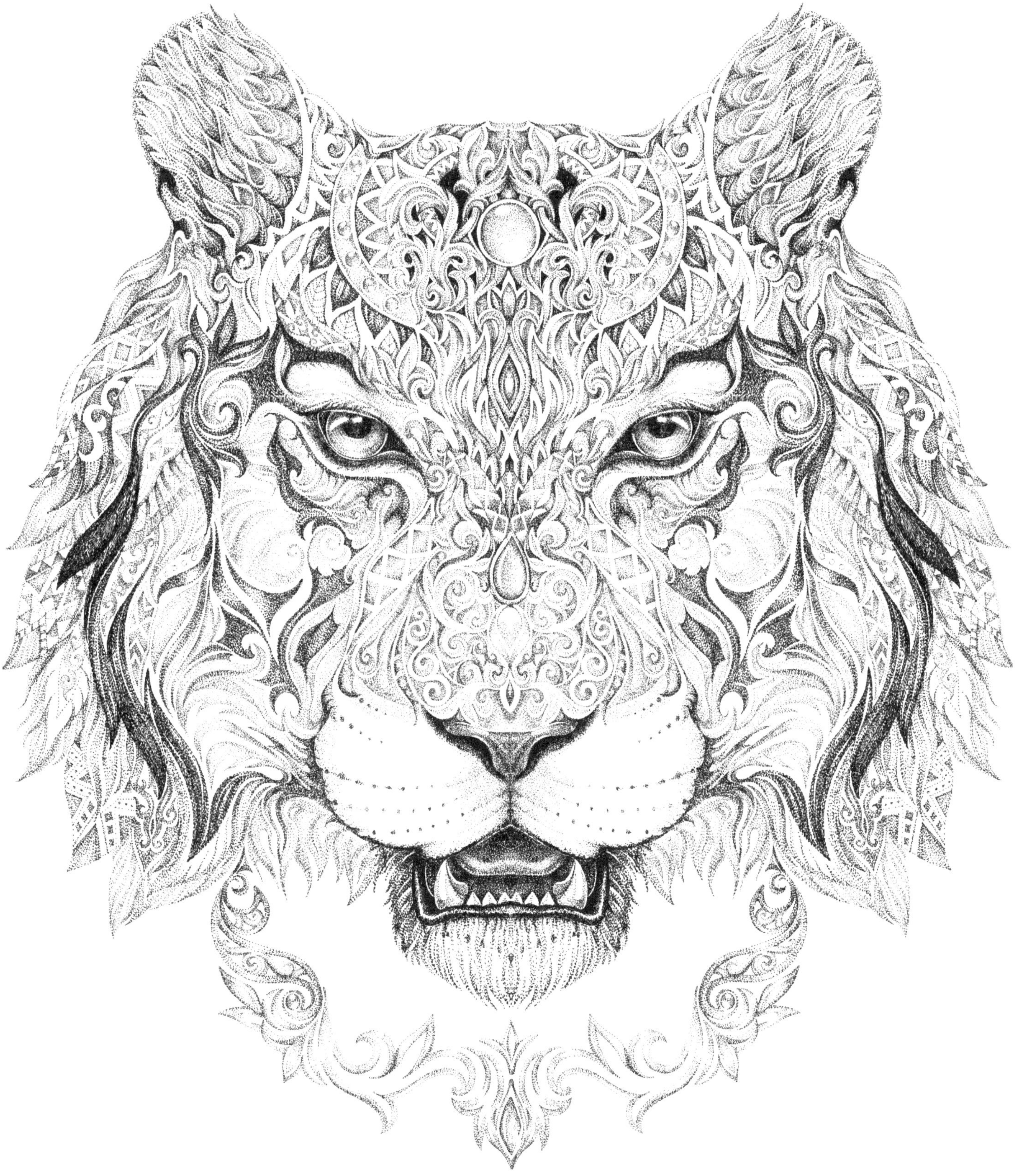

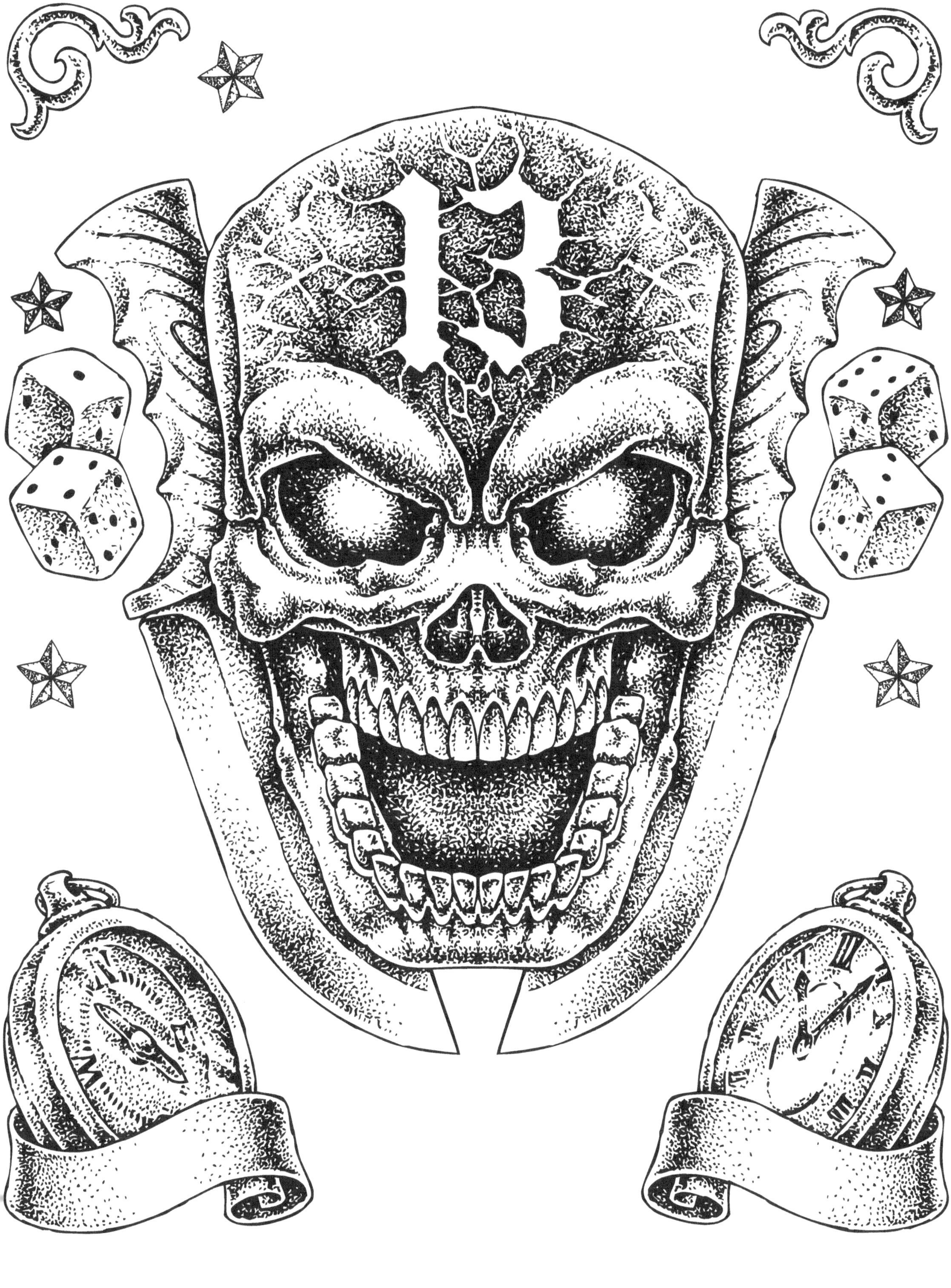

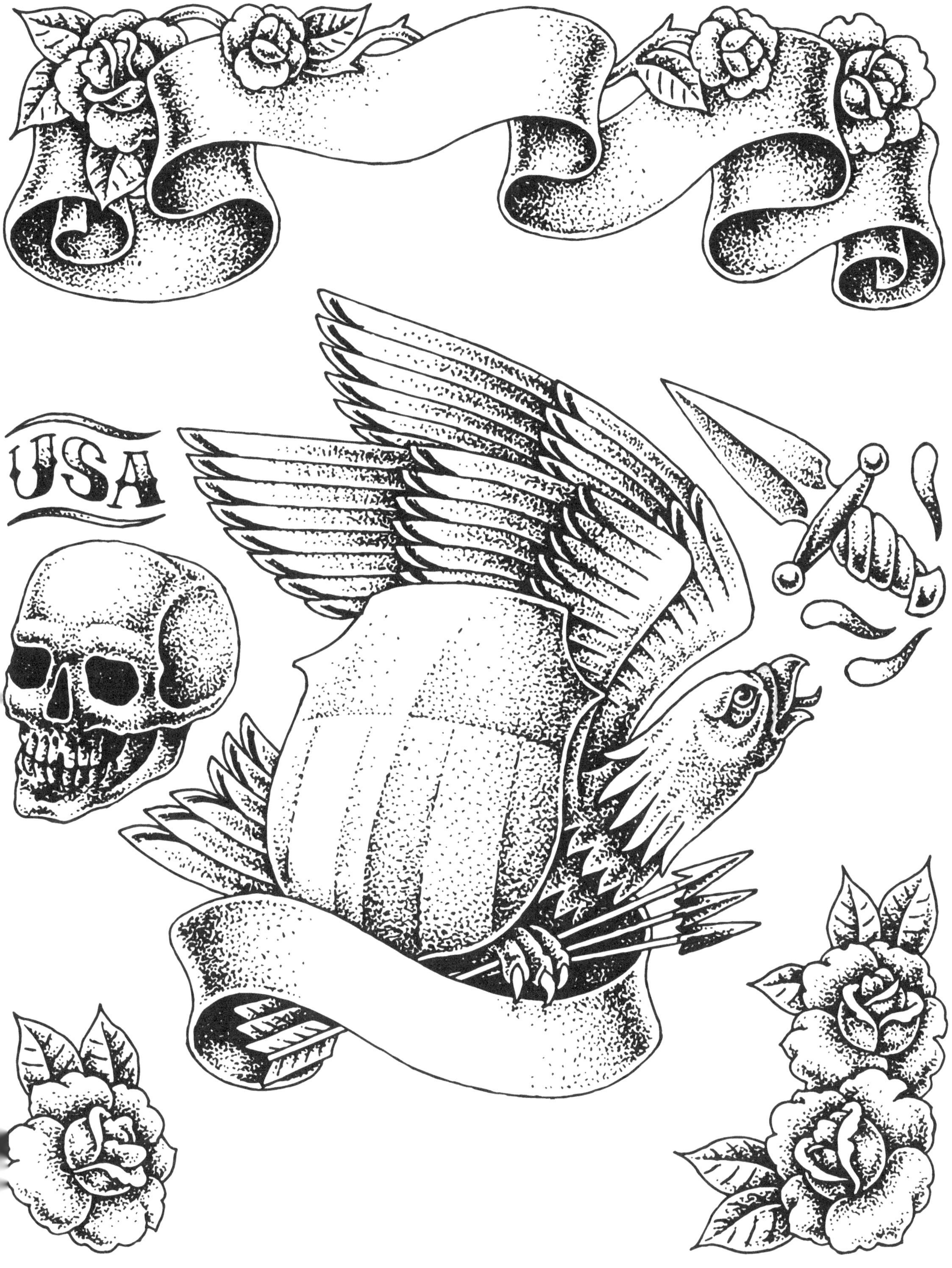
USA

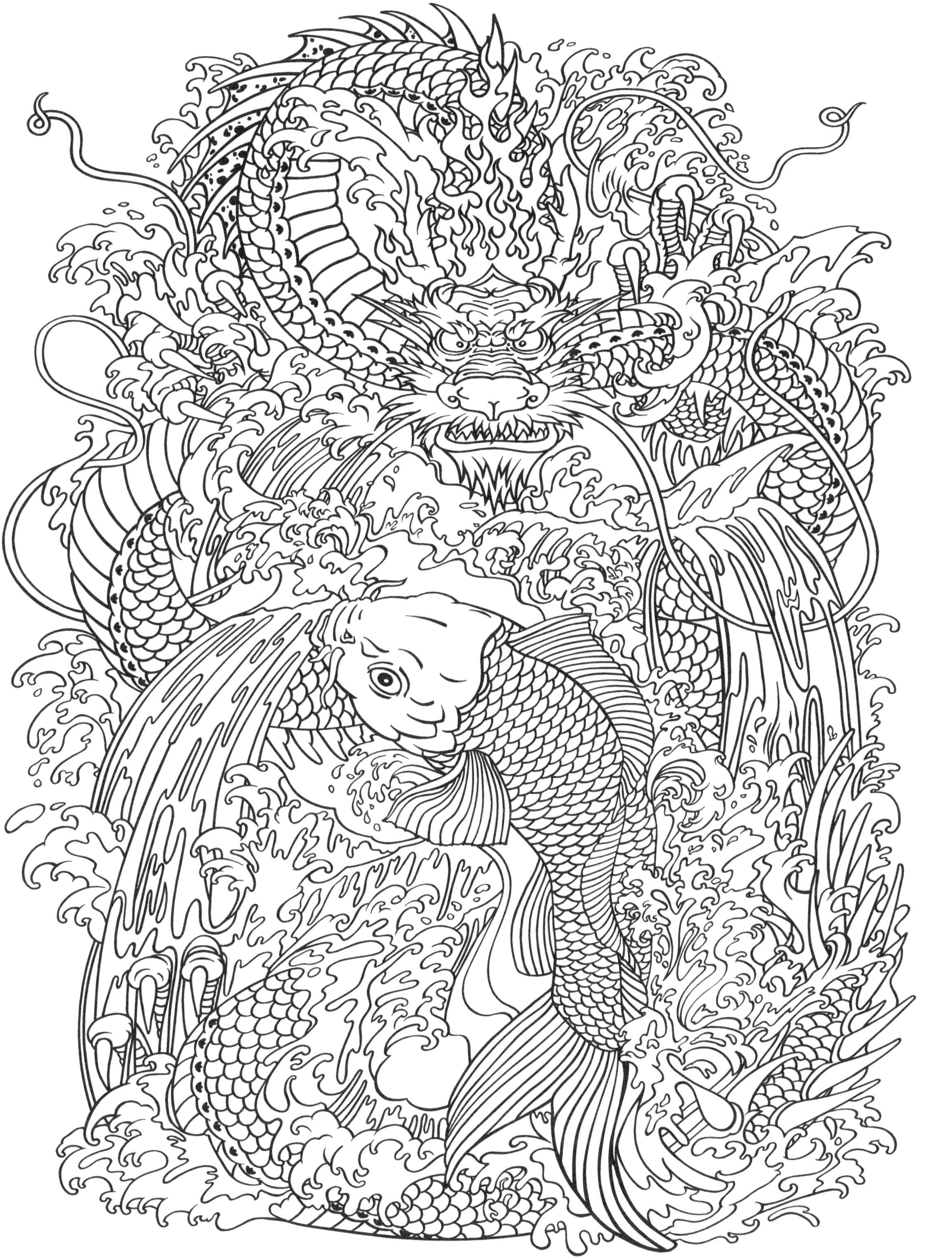

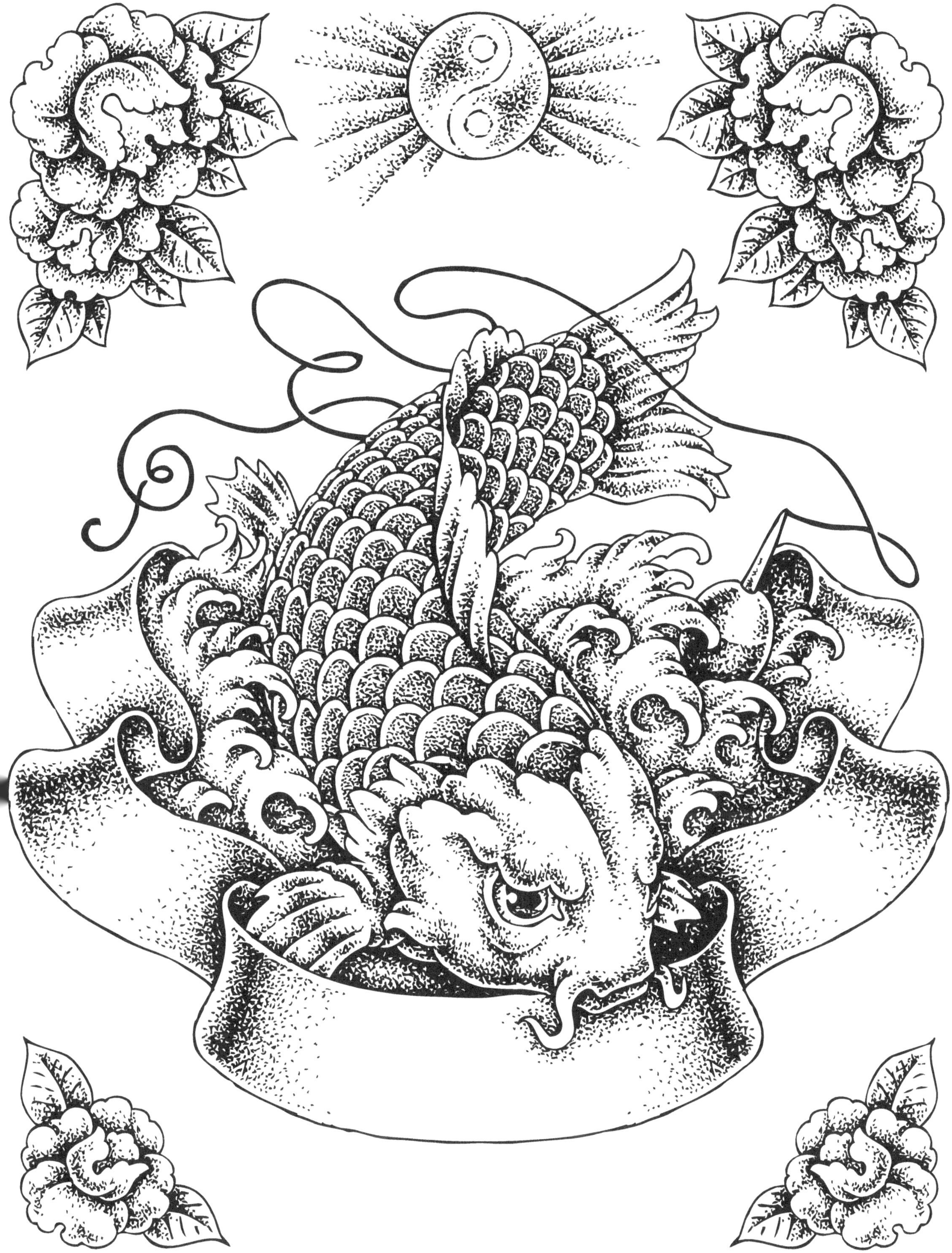

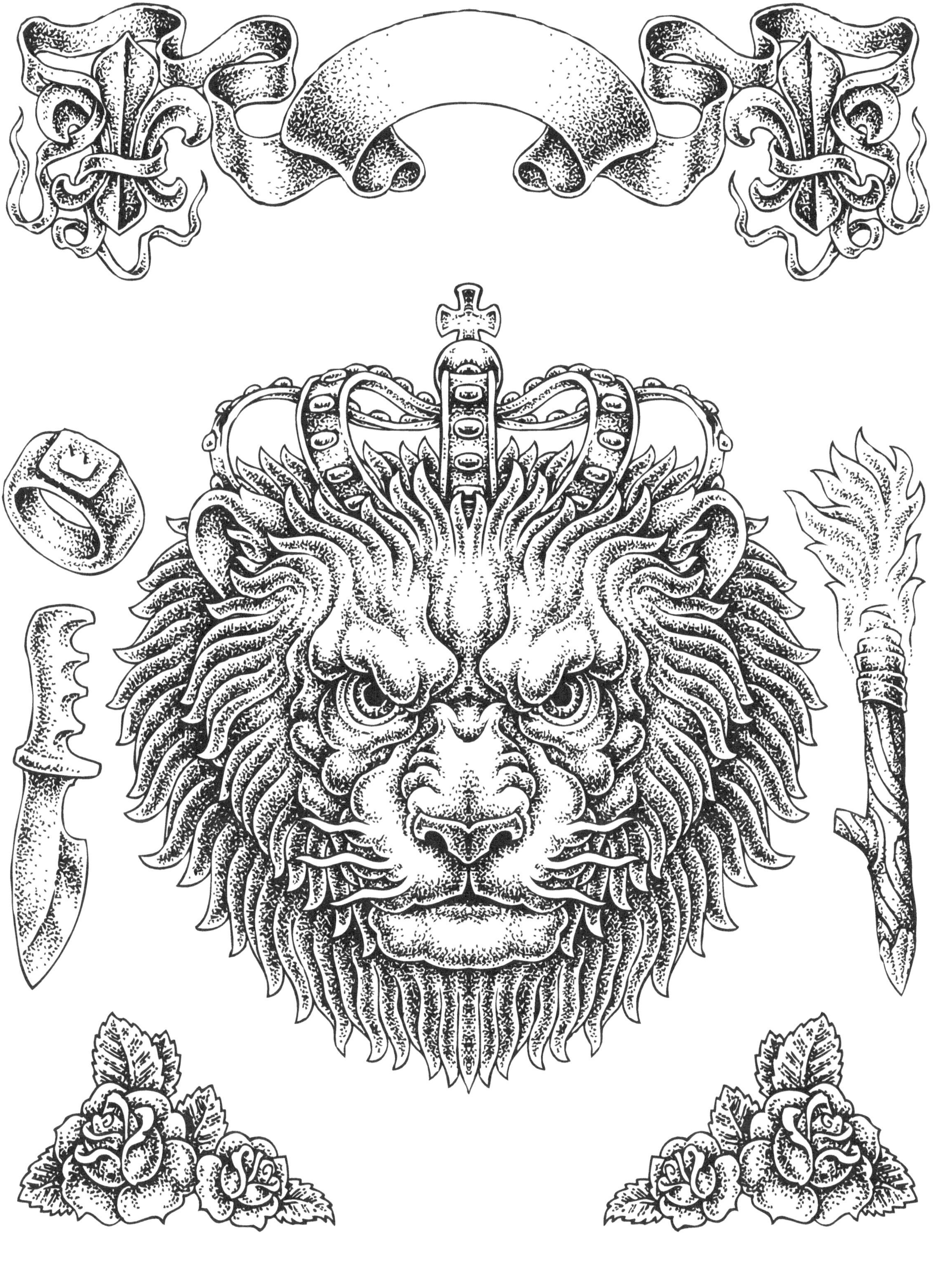

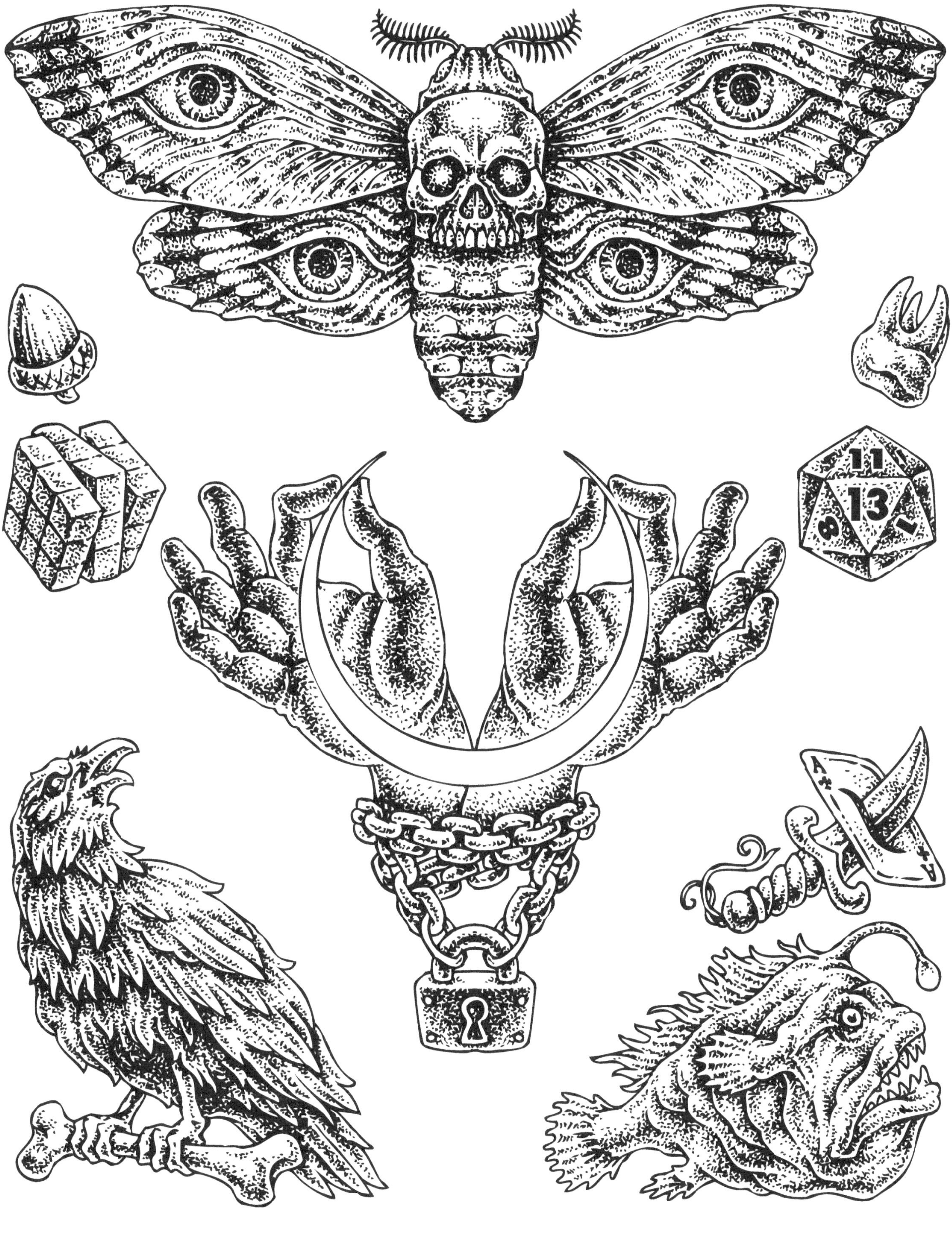
11
13

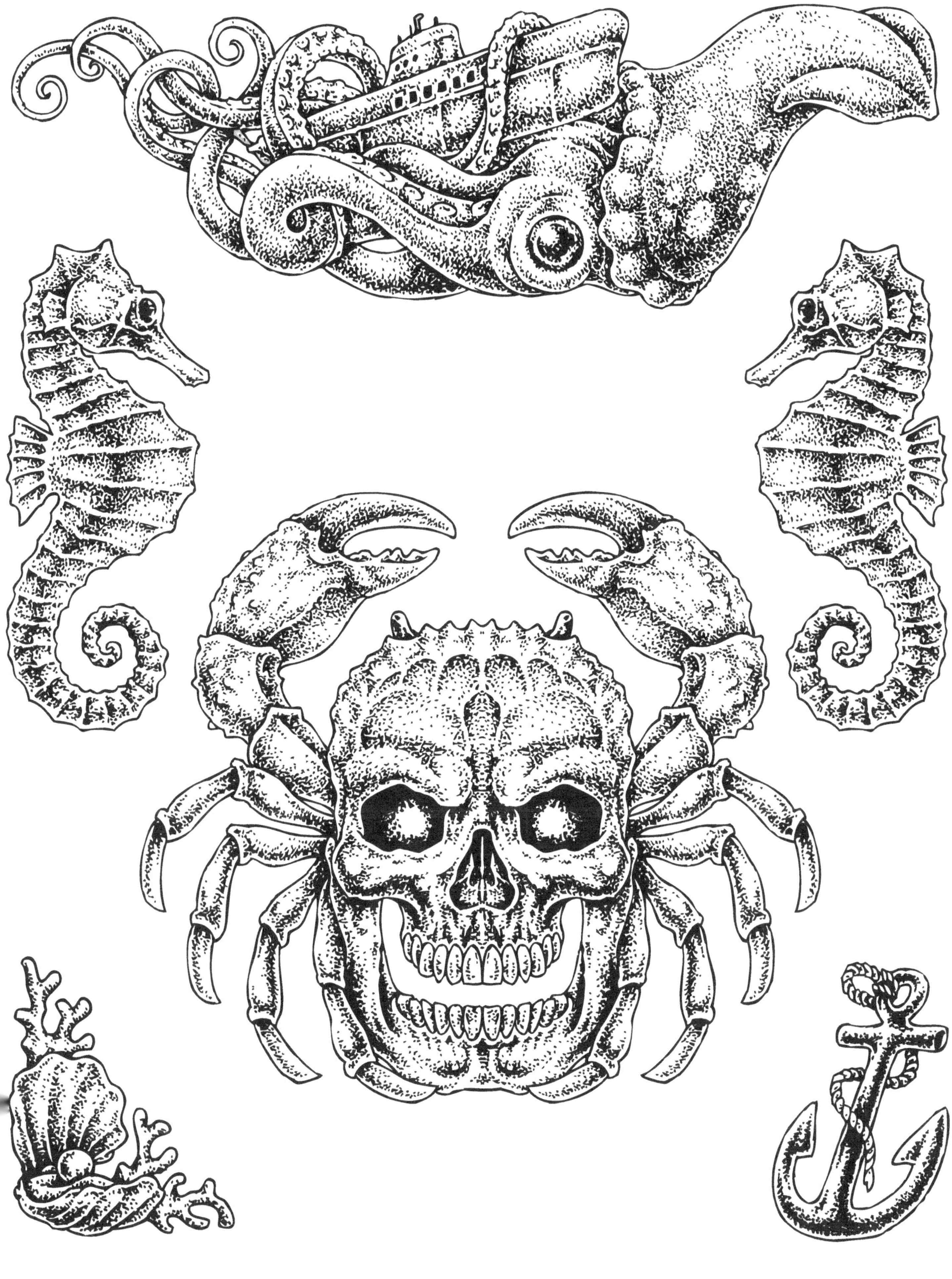

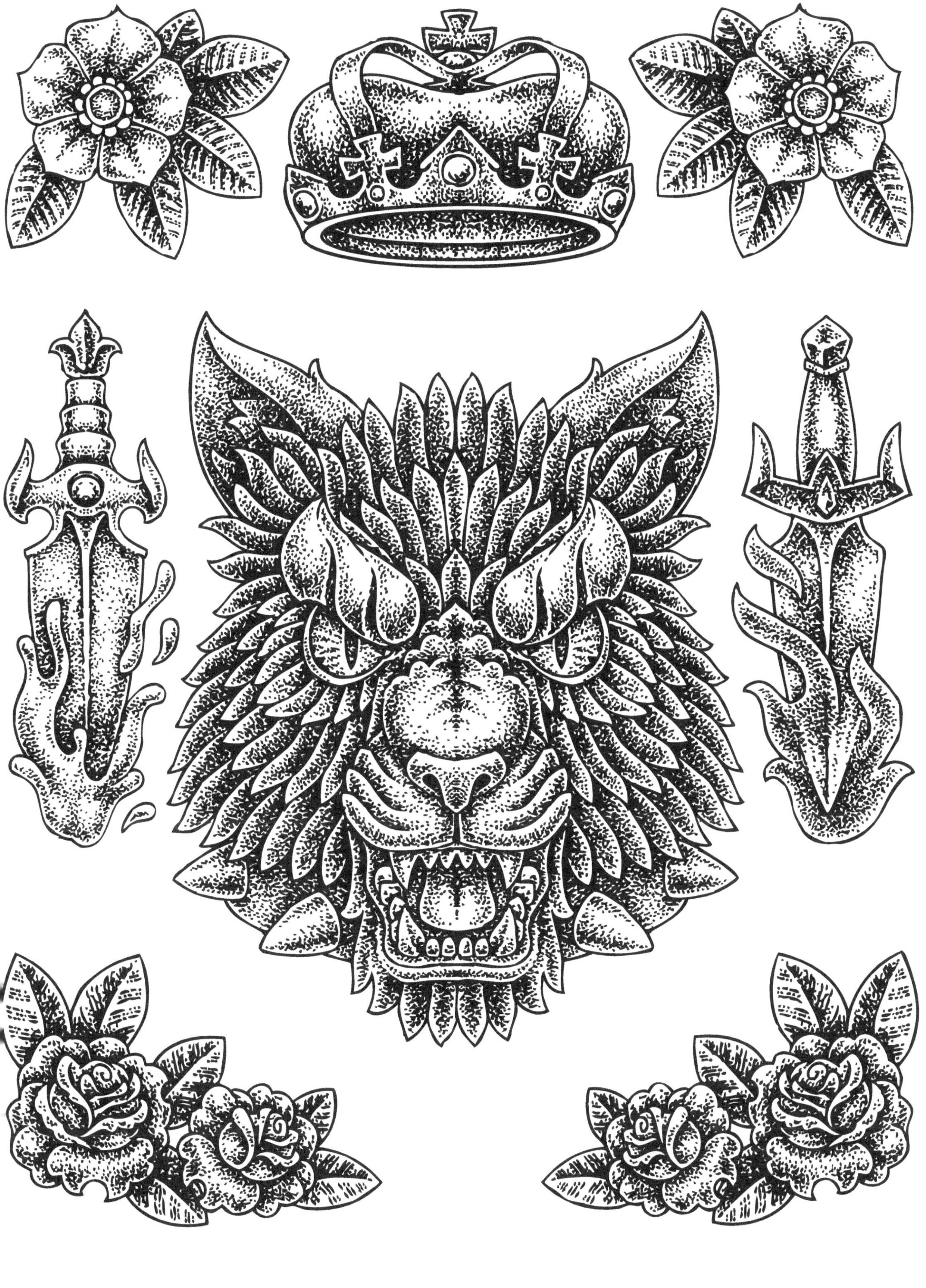

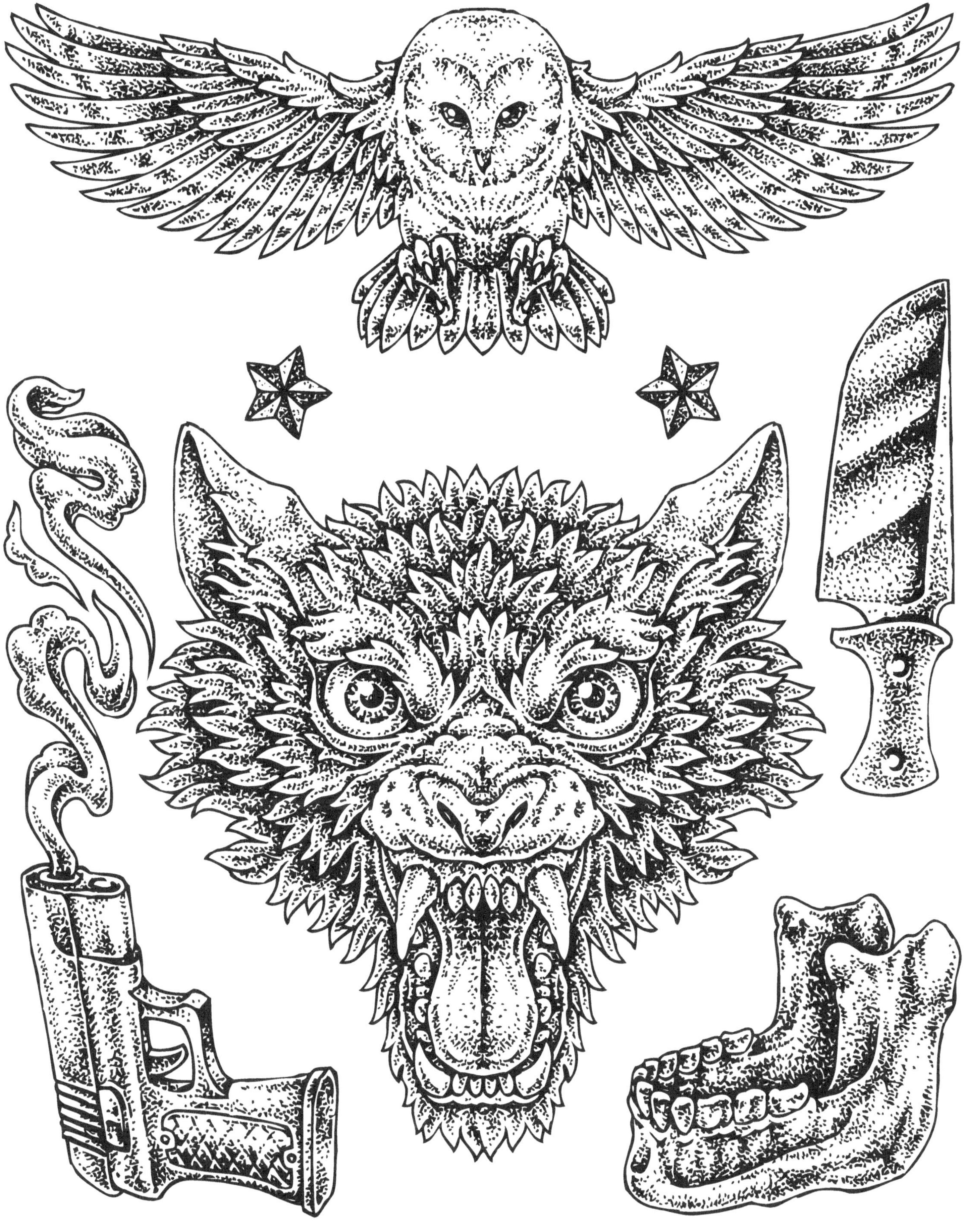

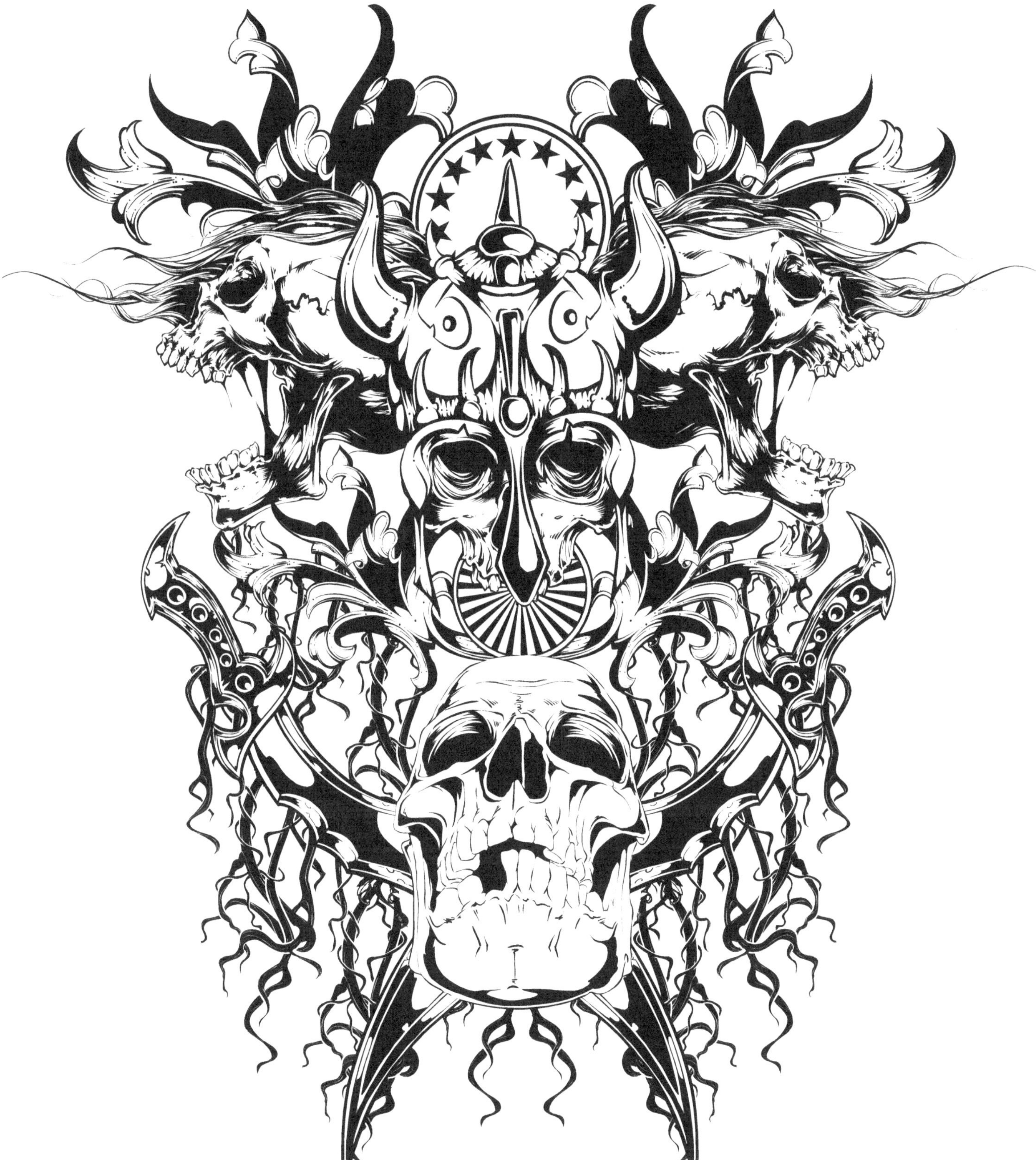

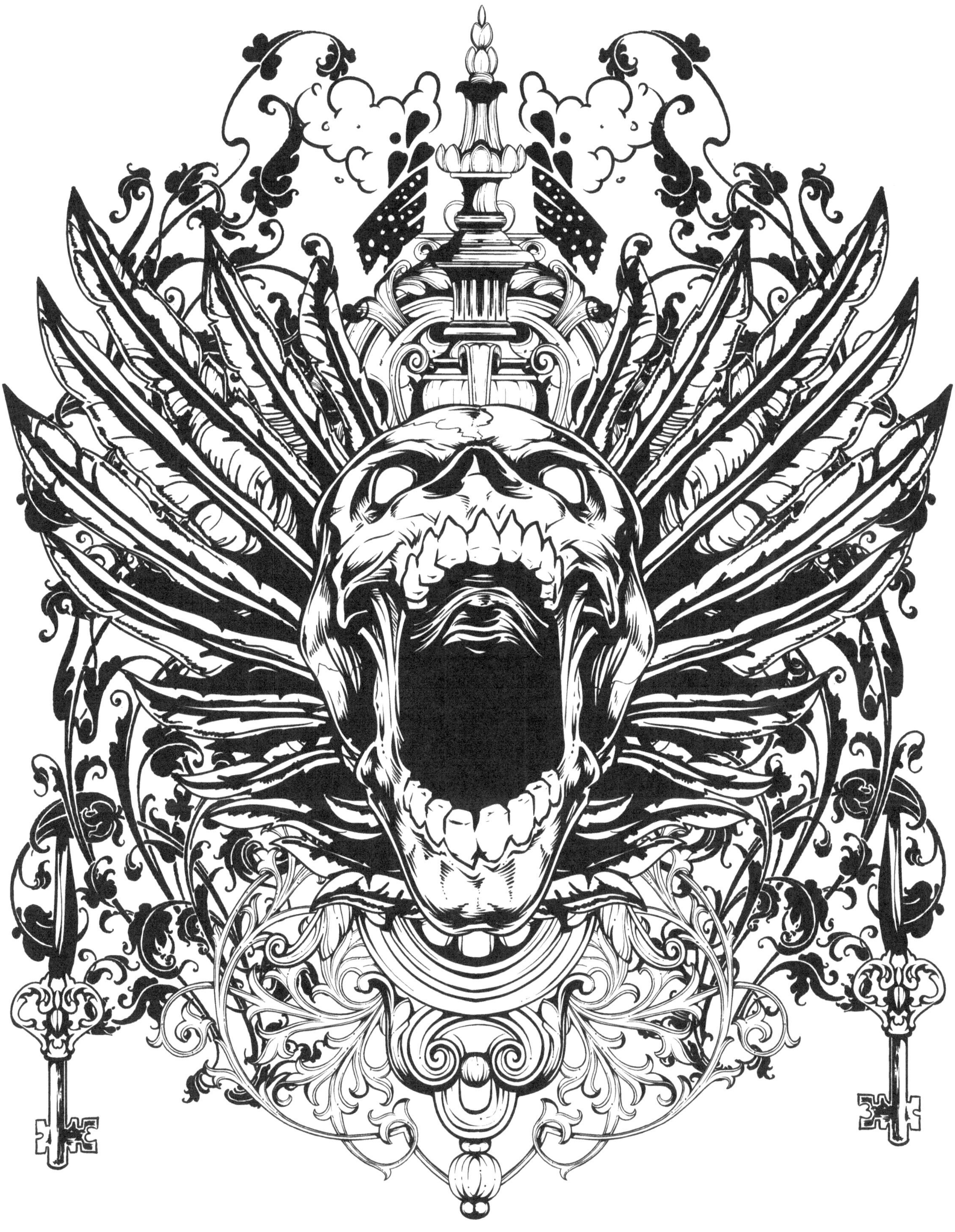

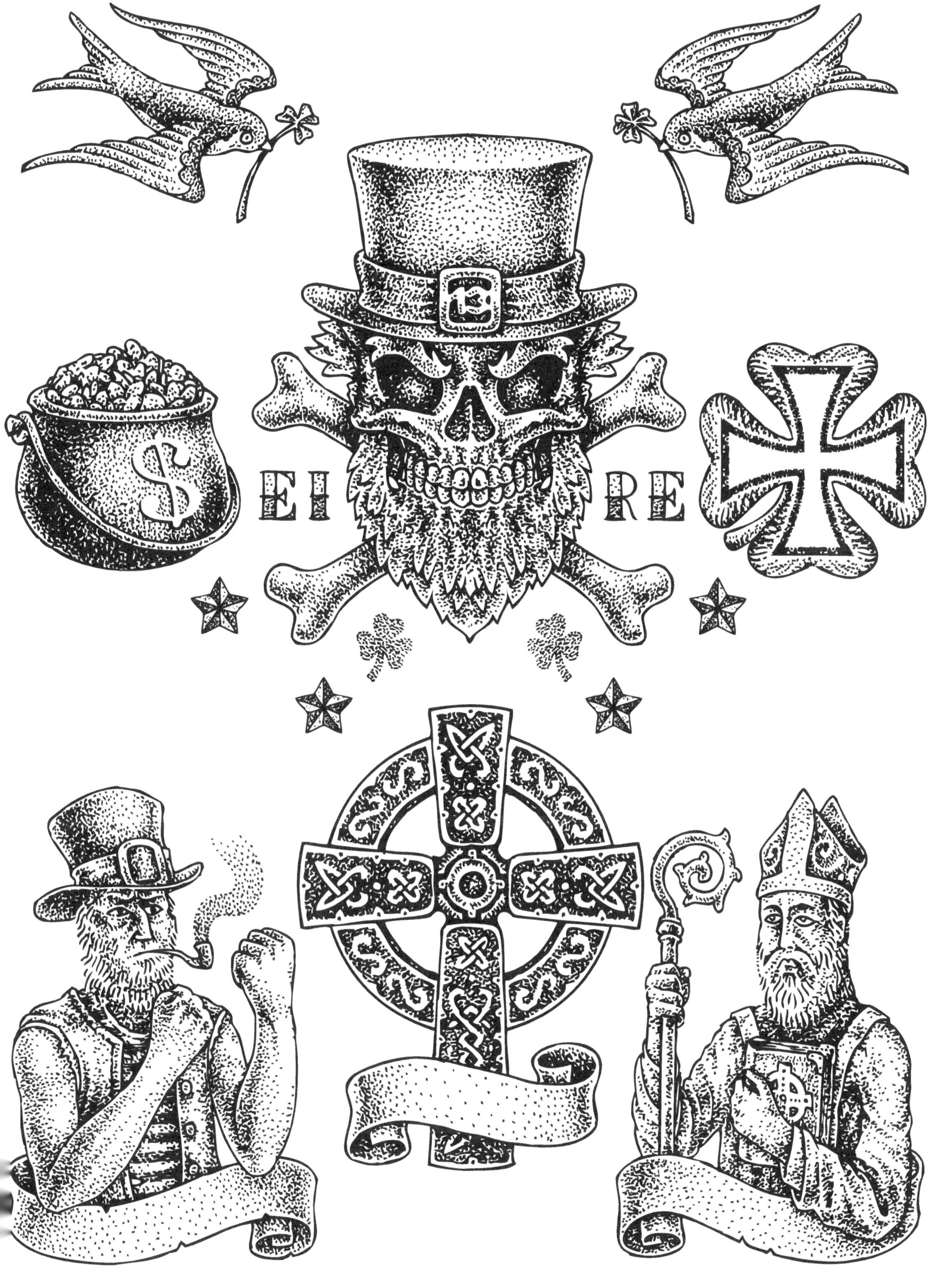
EI
RE

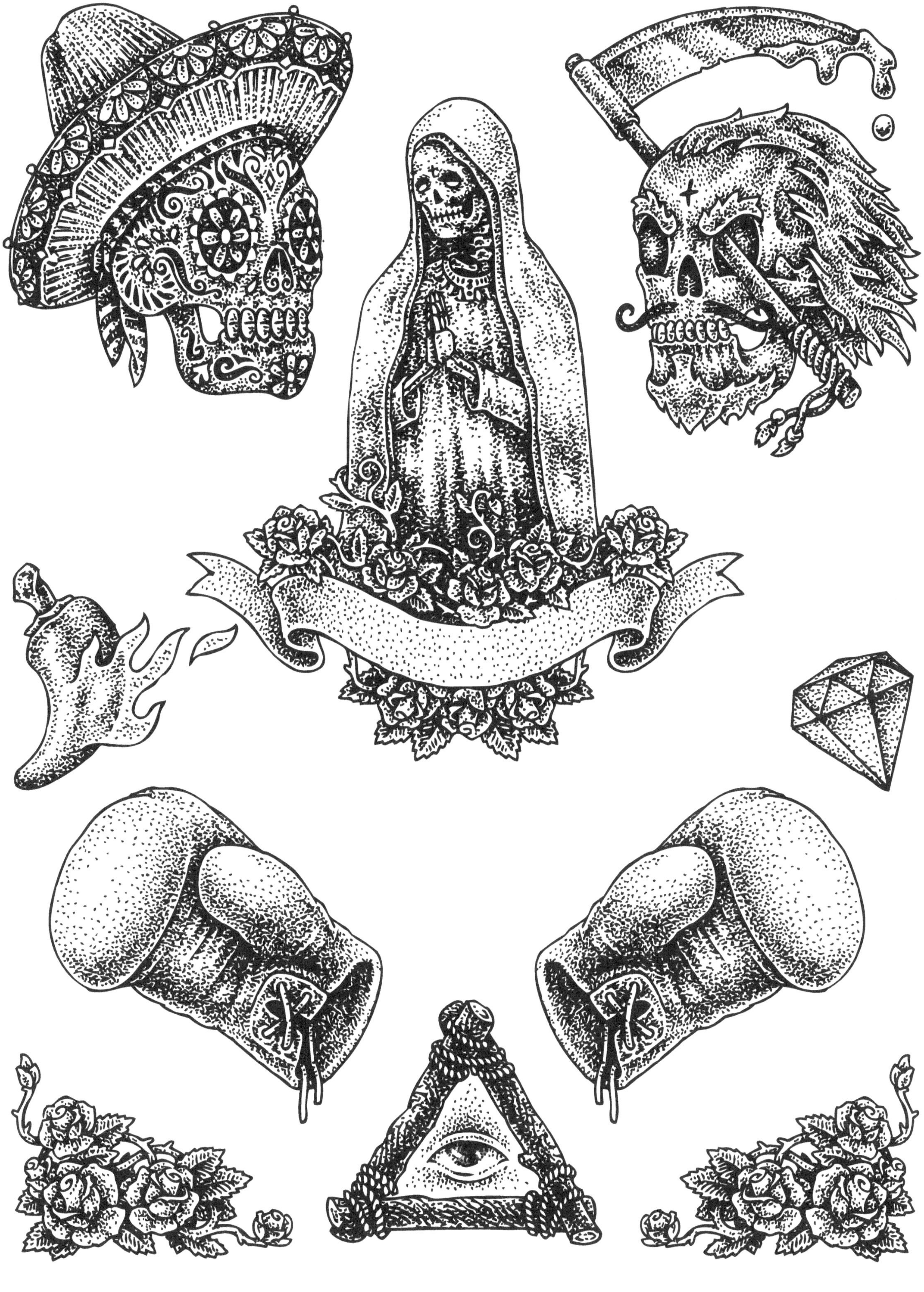

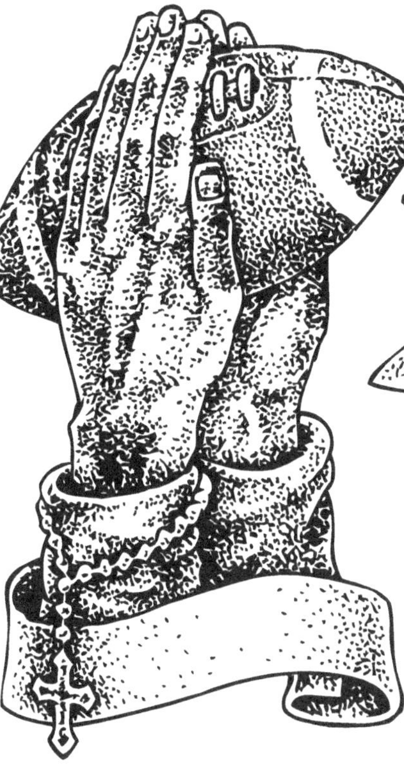

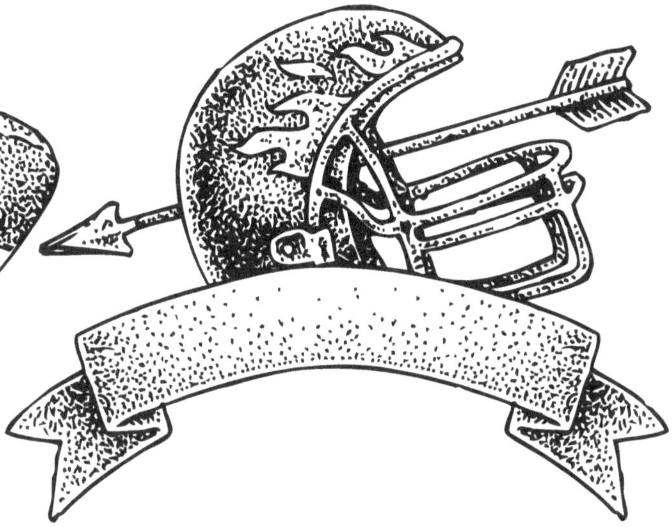

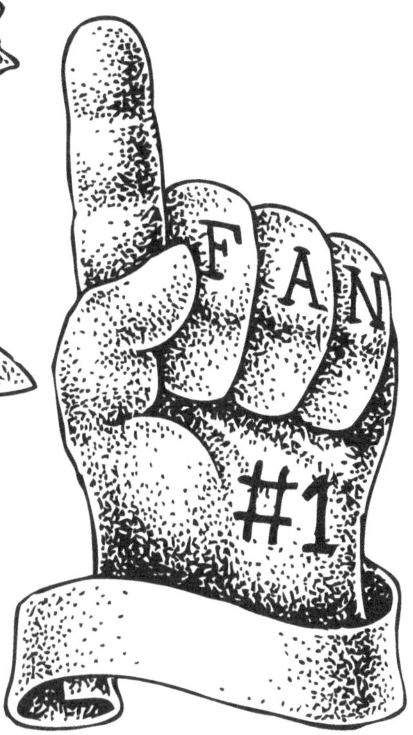
FAN
#1

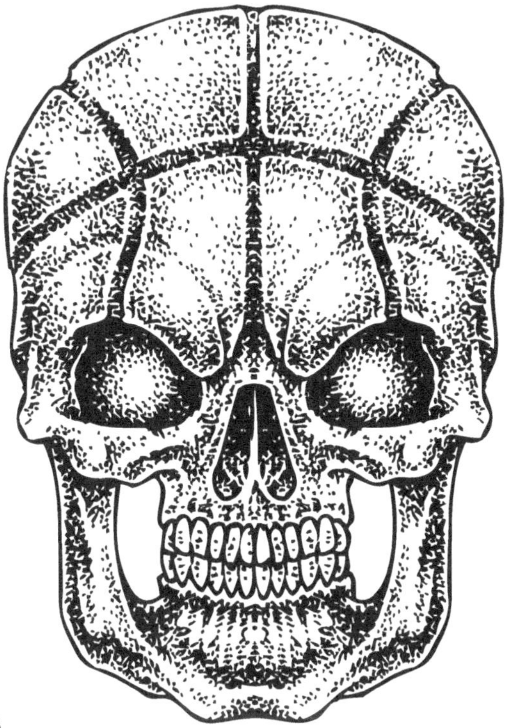

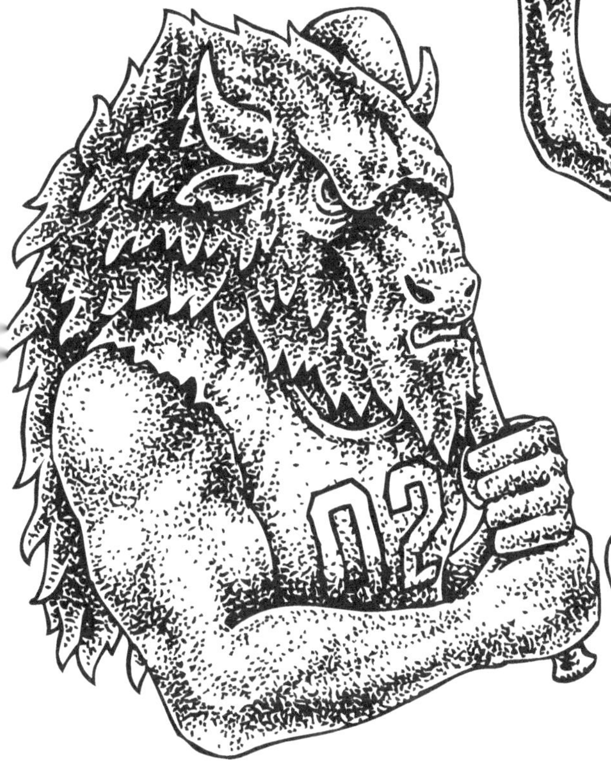
02

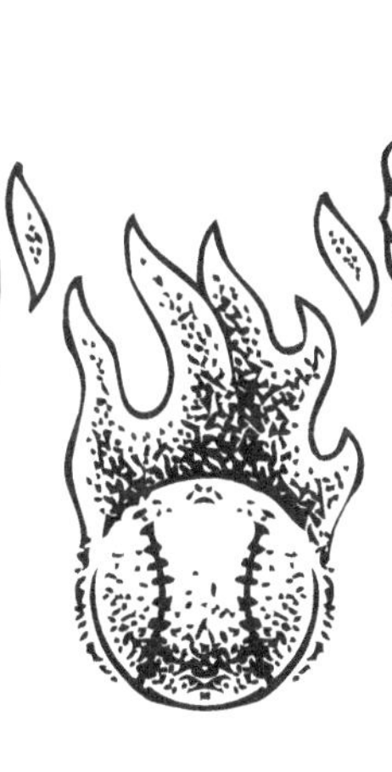

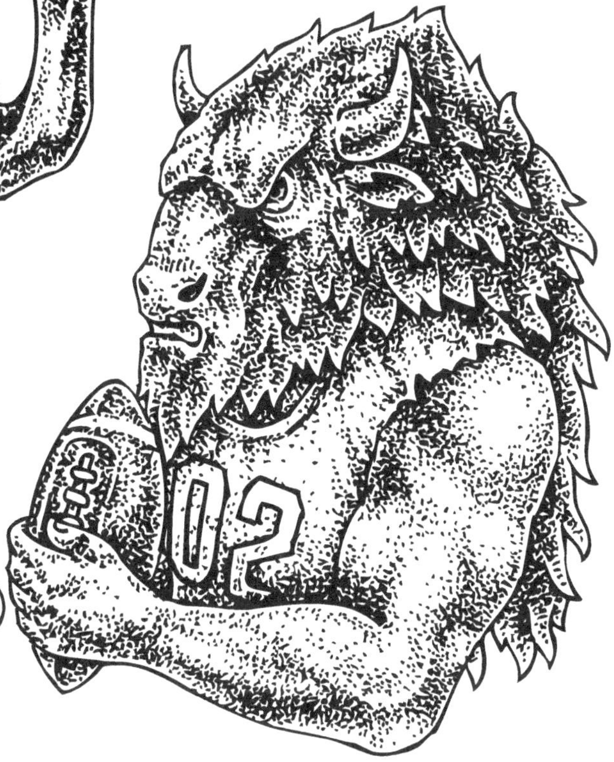
02

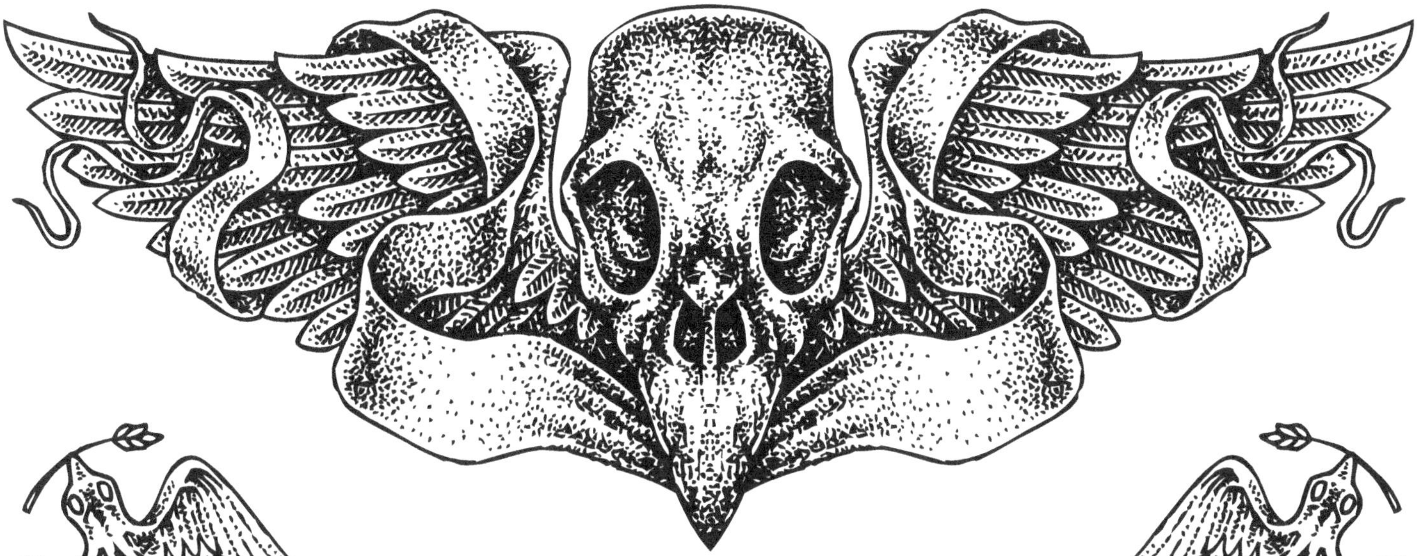
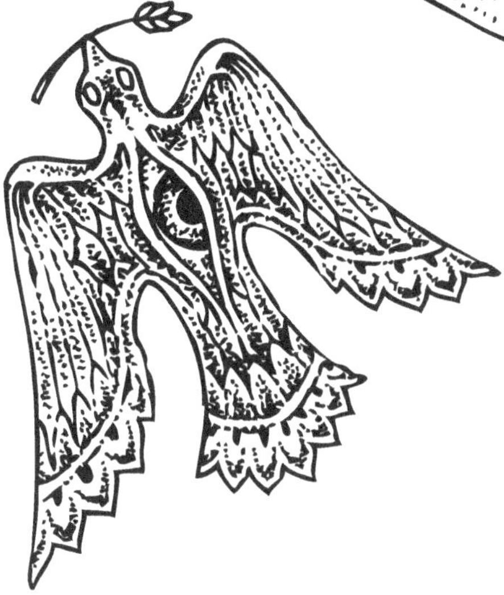
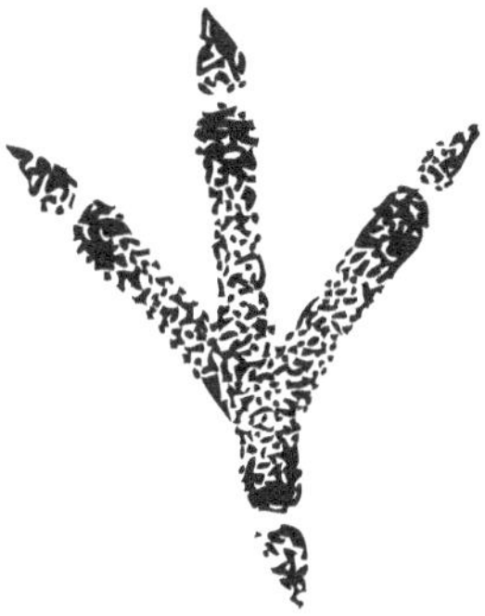
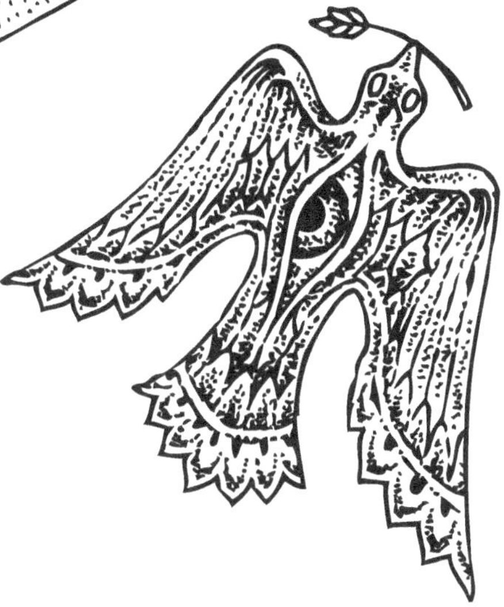
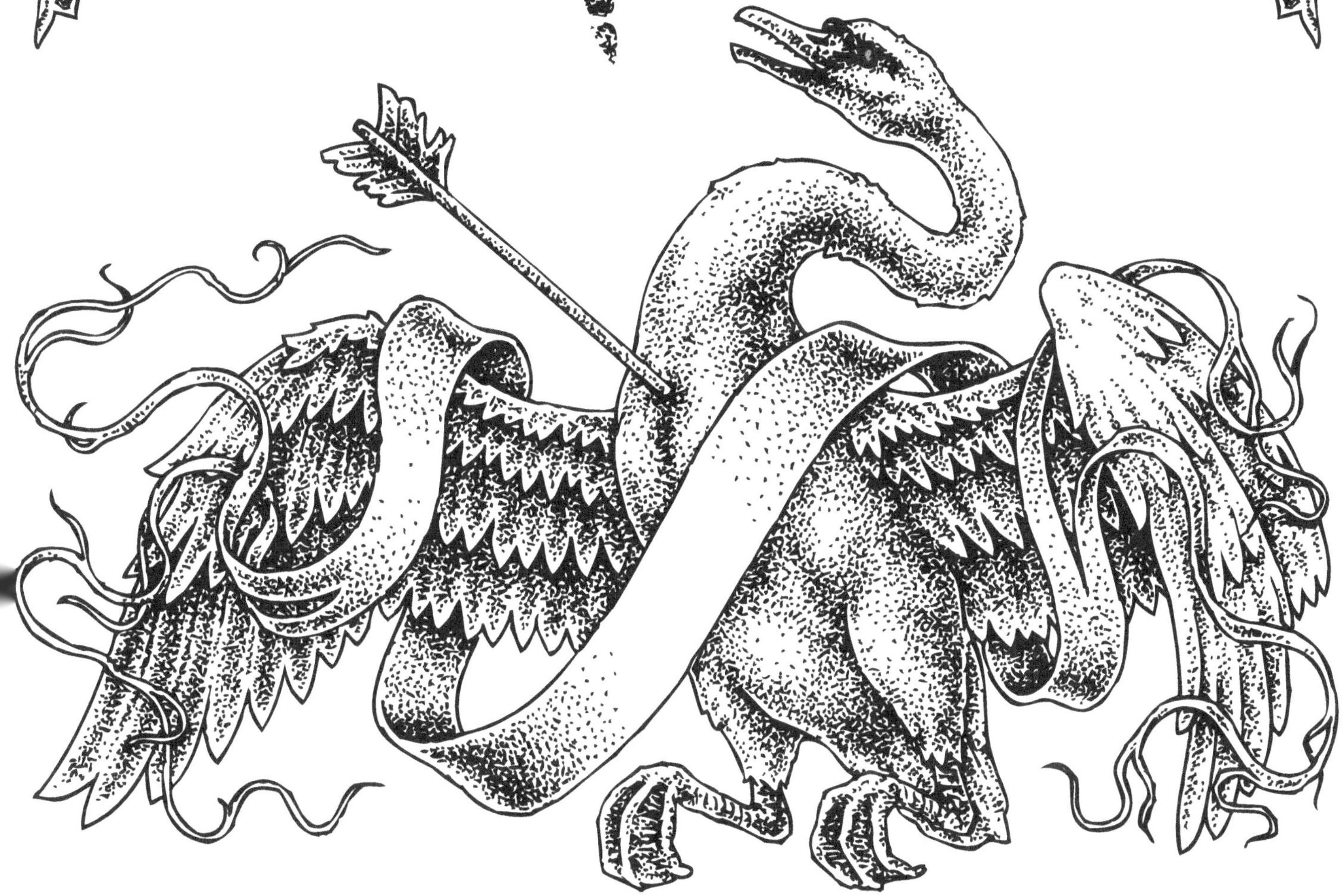

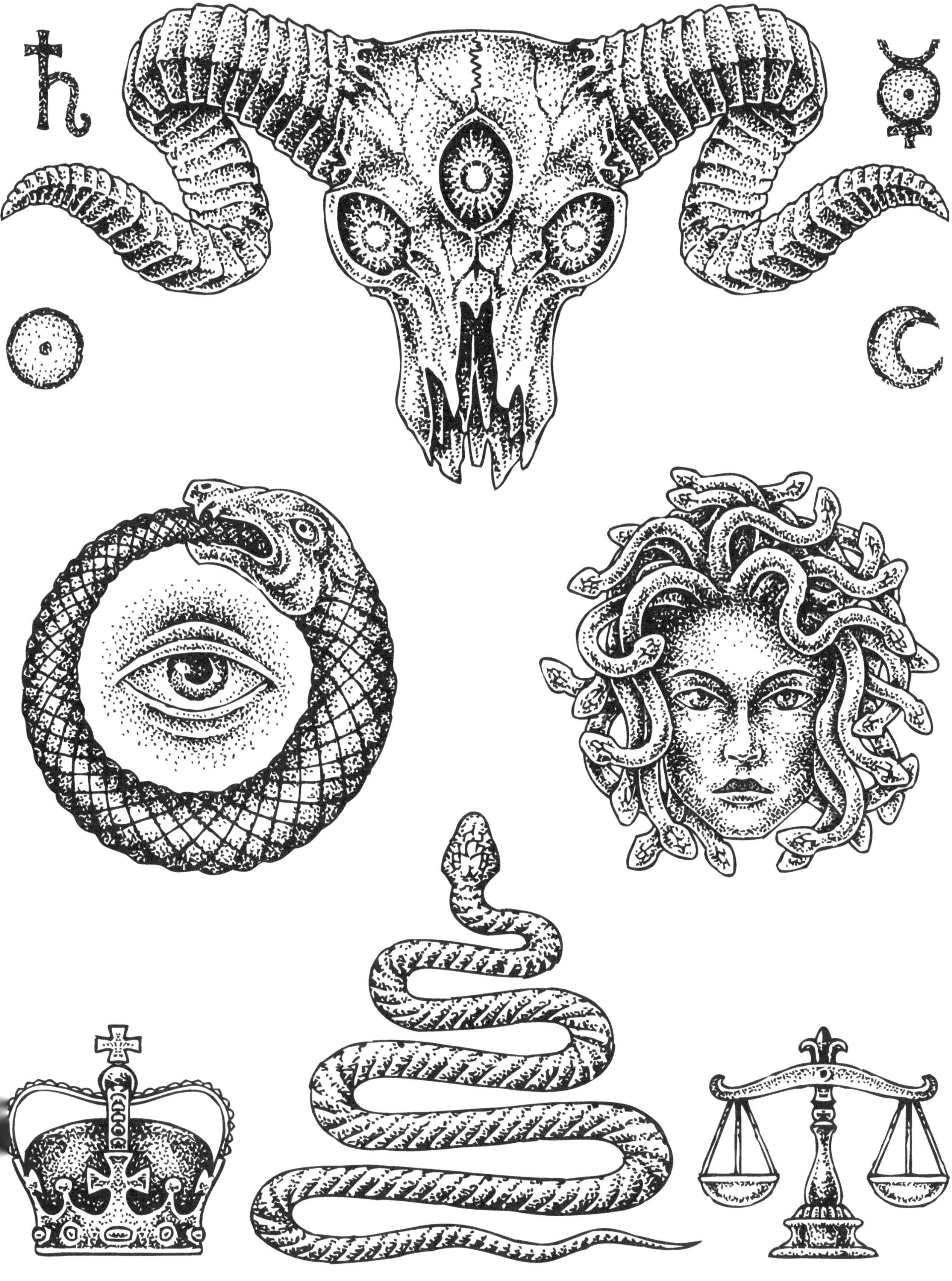

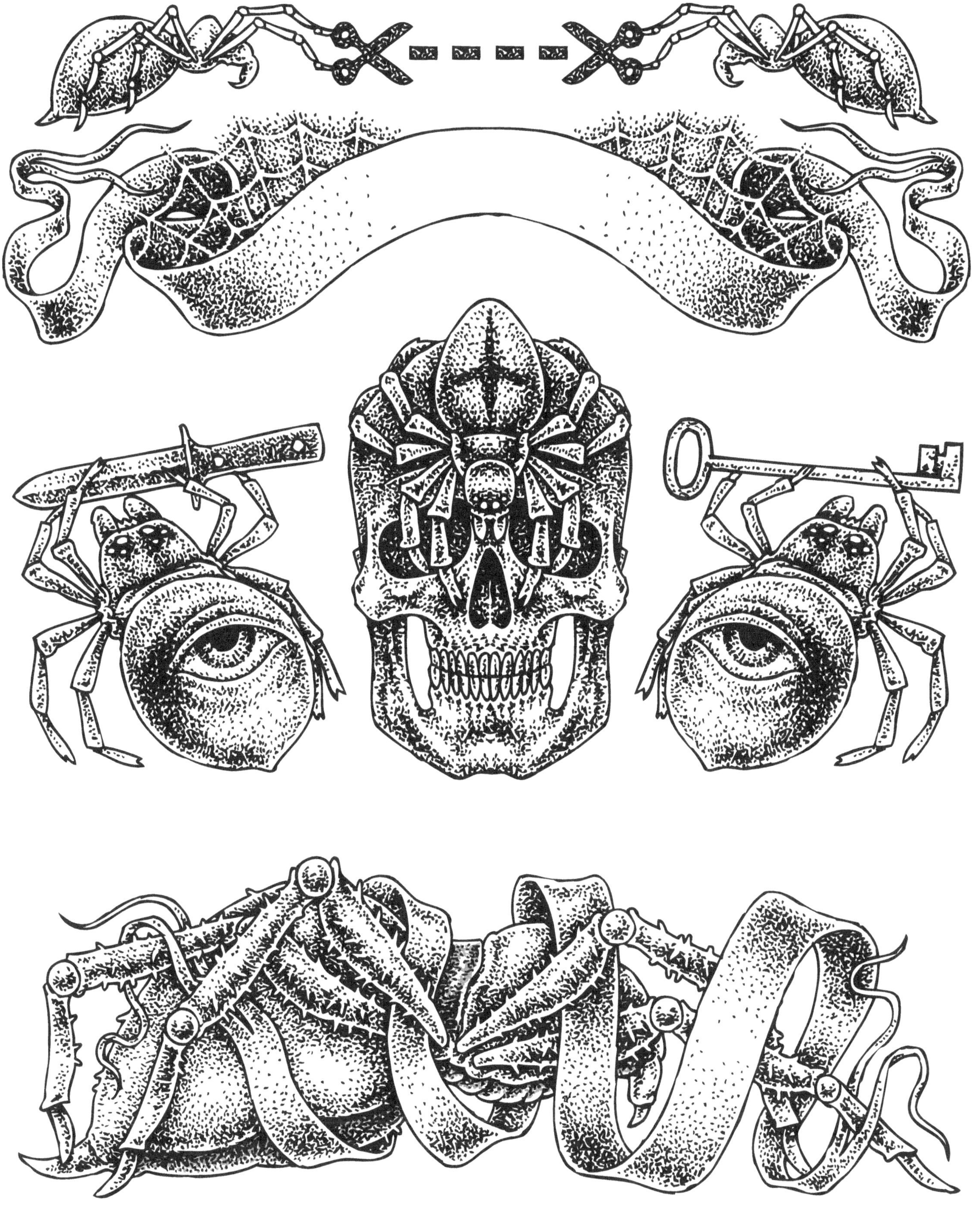

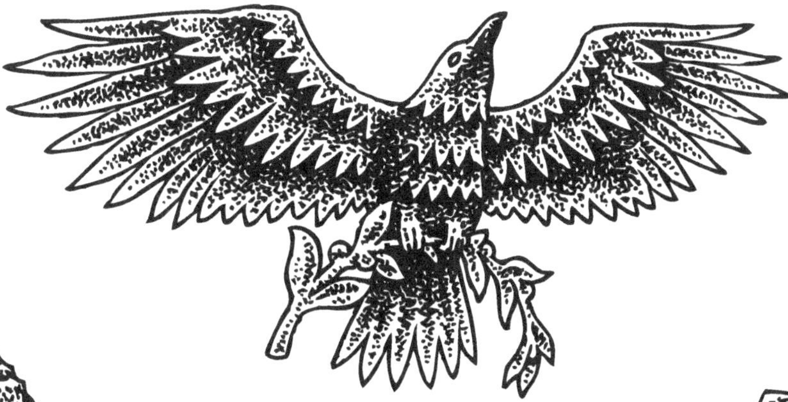
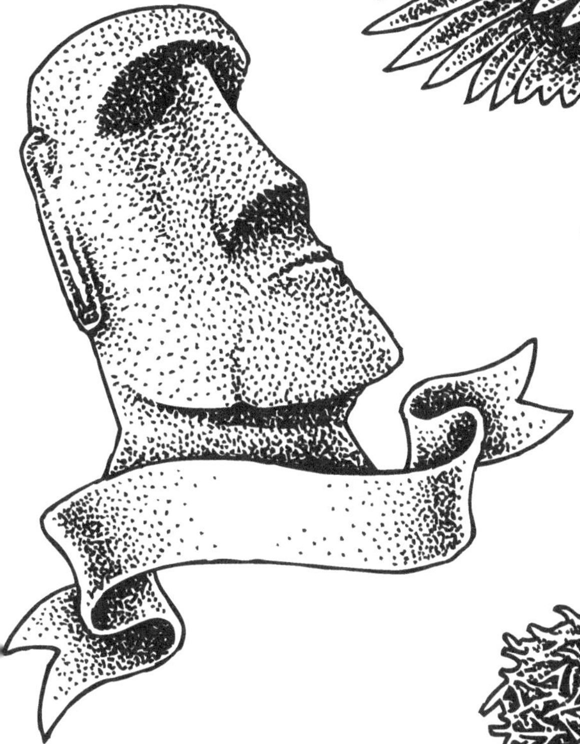
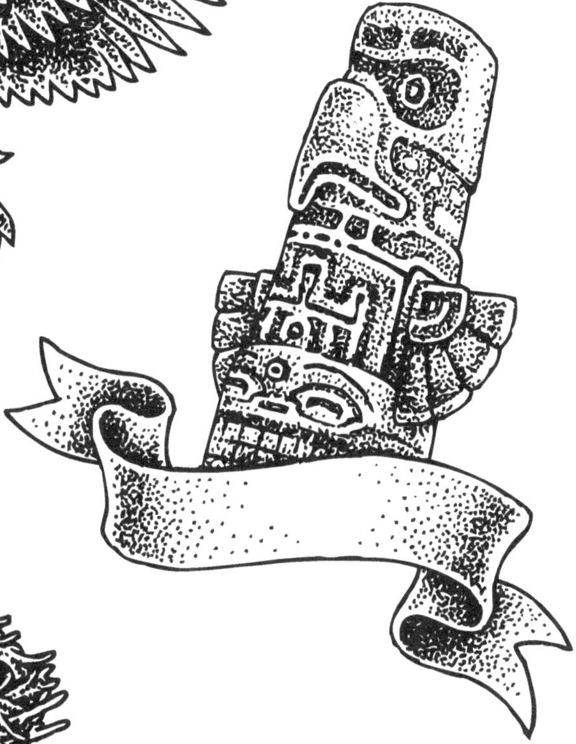
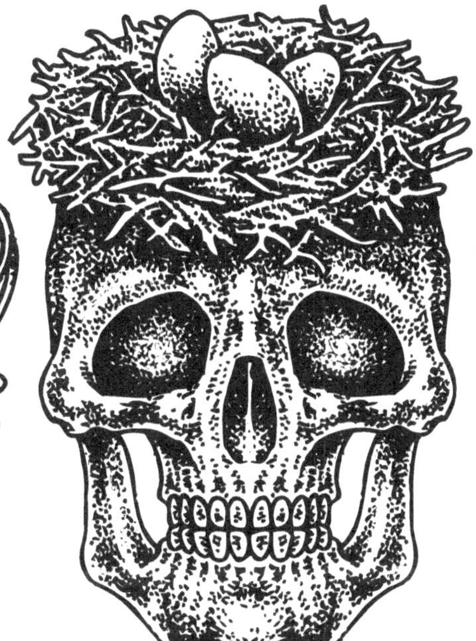
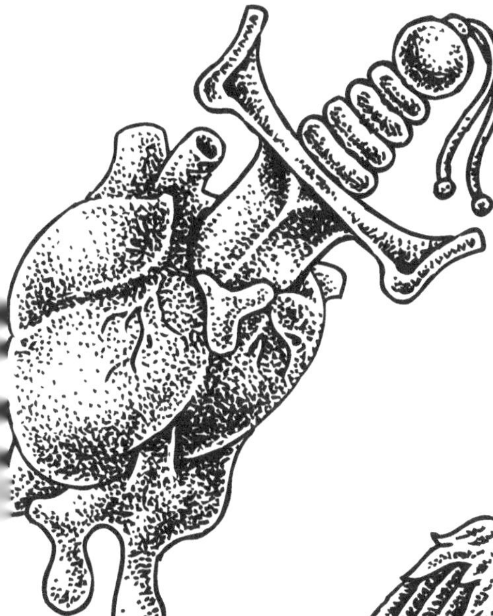
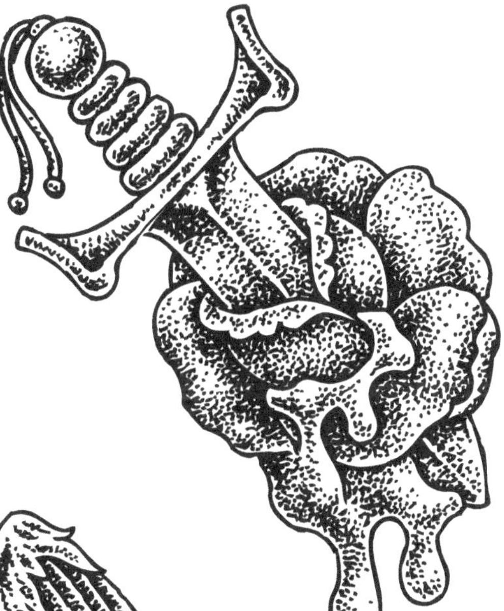
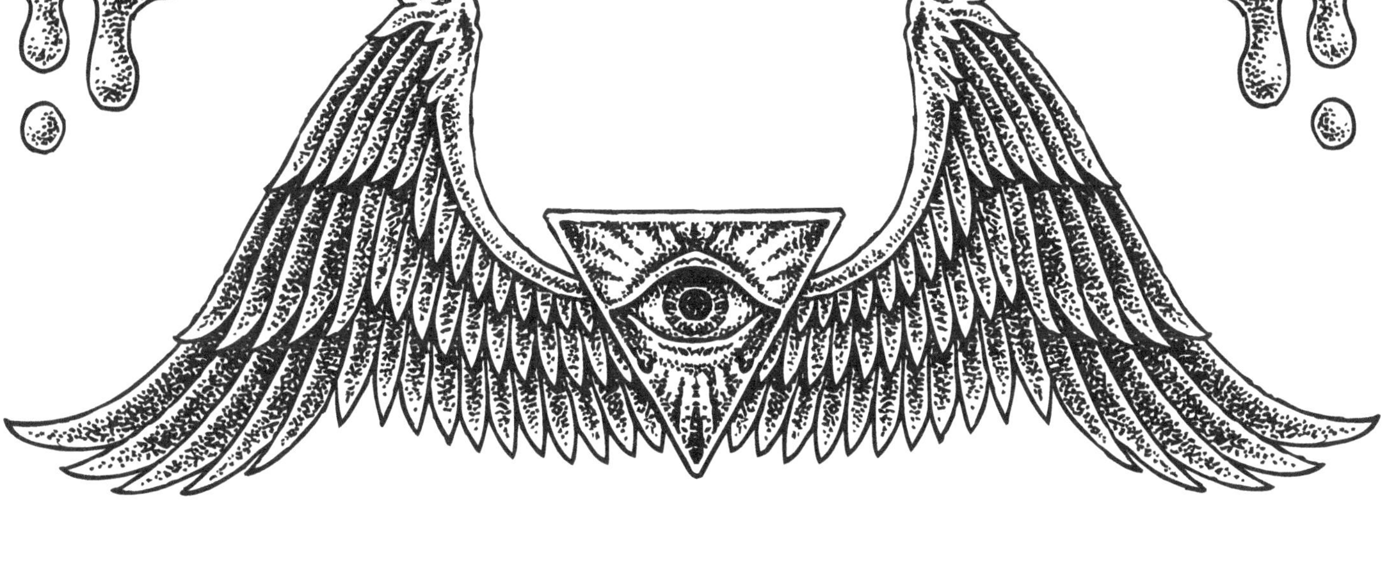

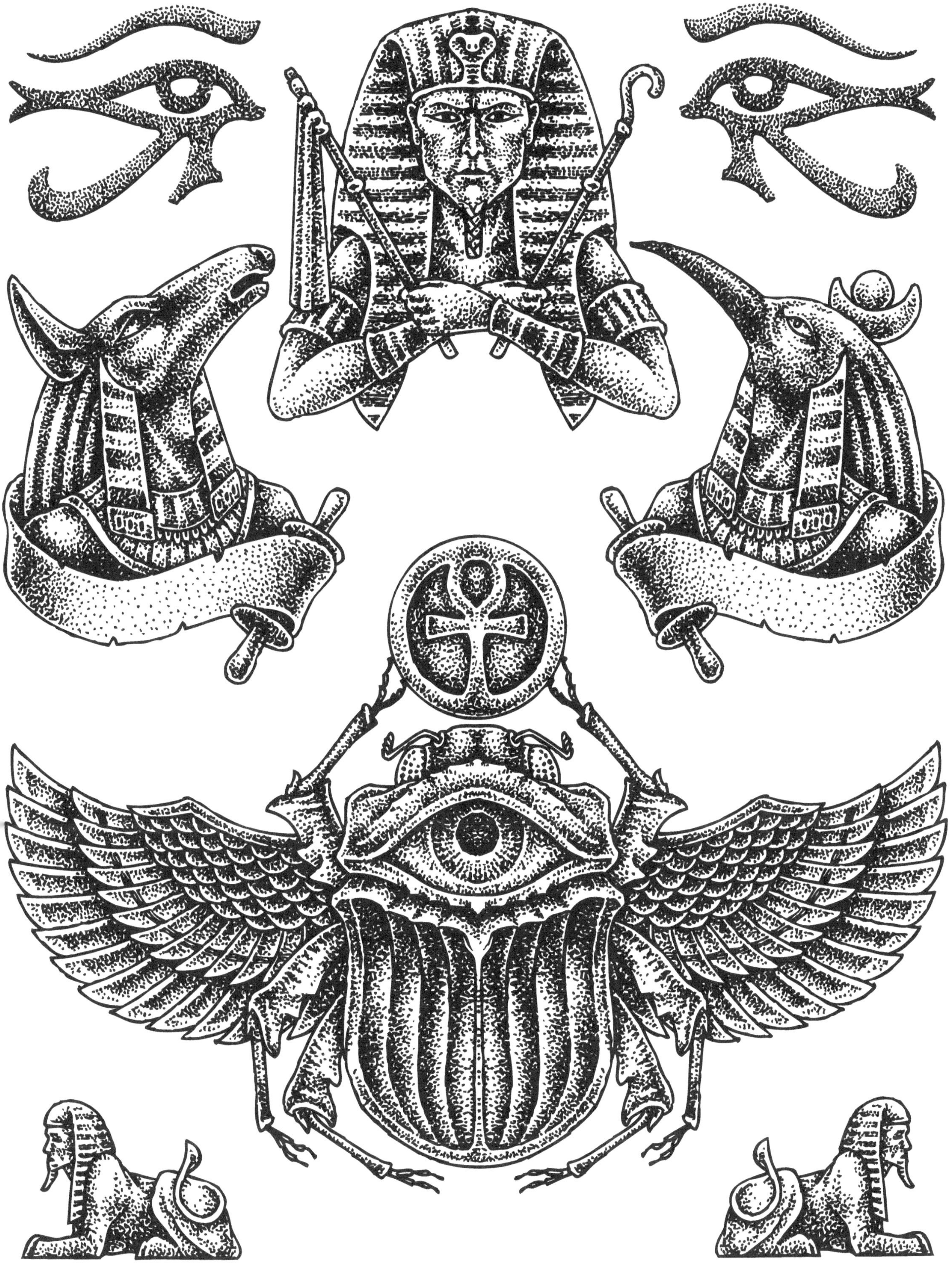

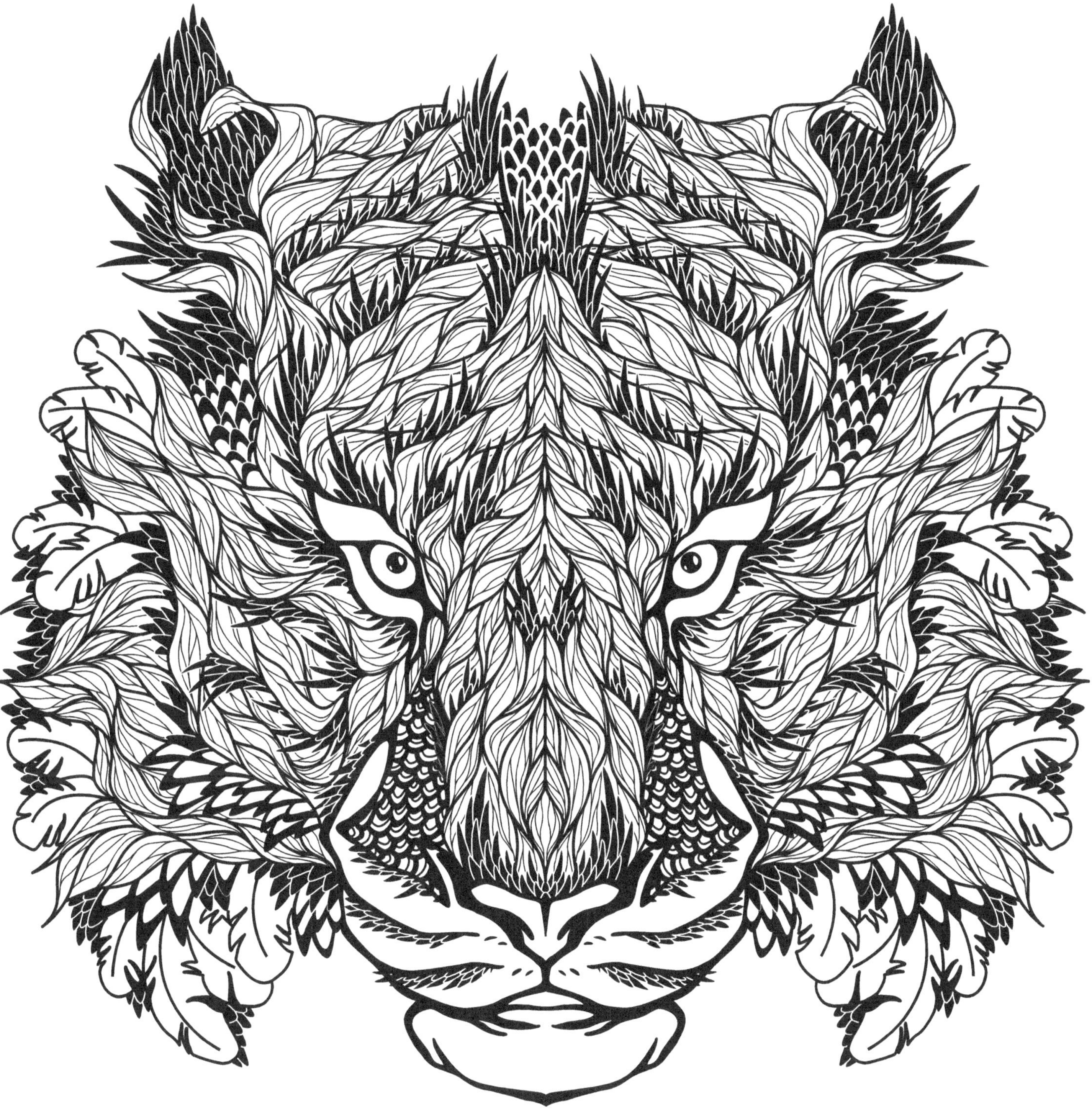

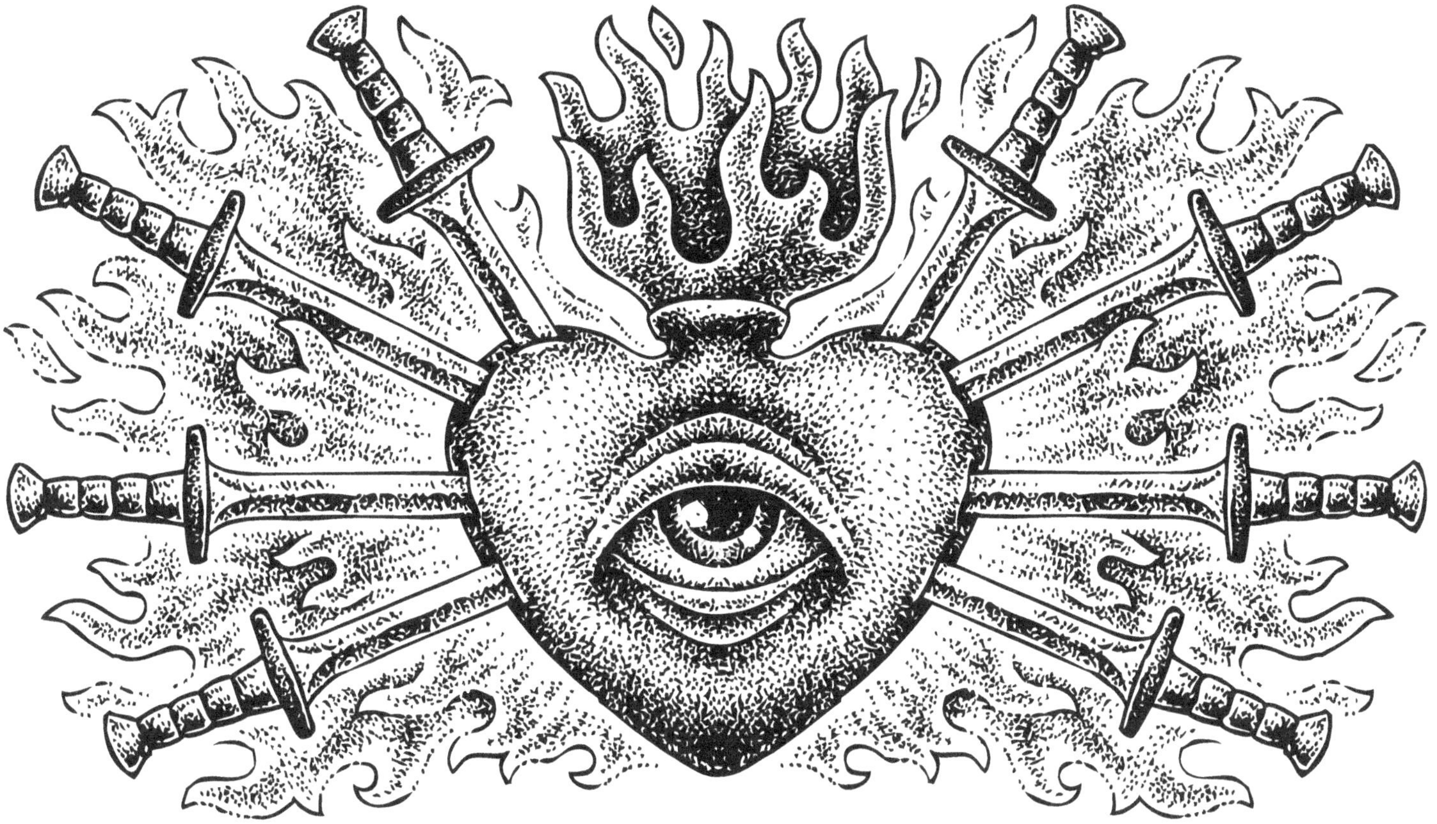

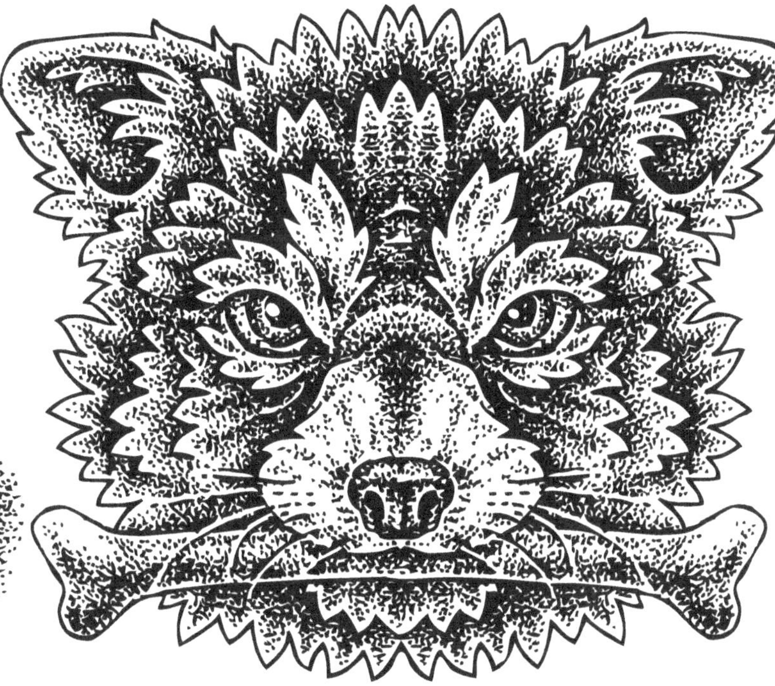

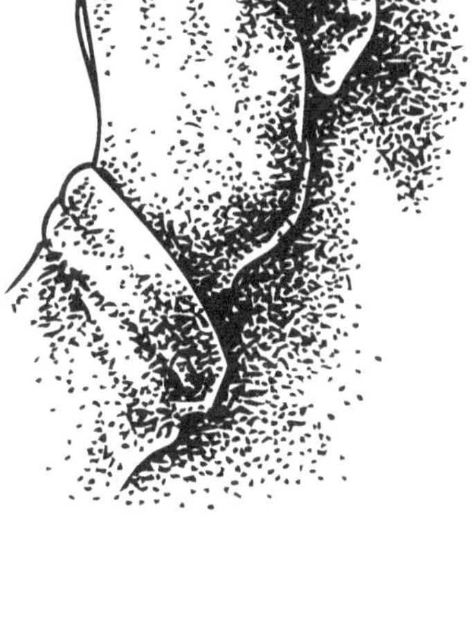

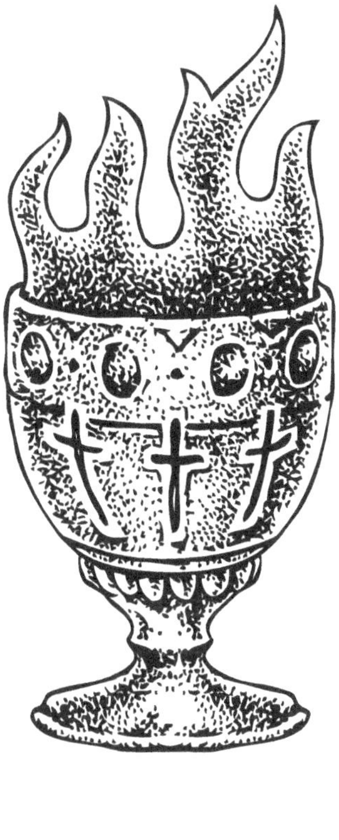

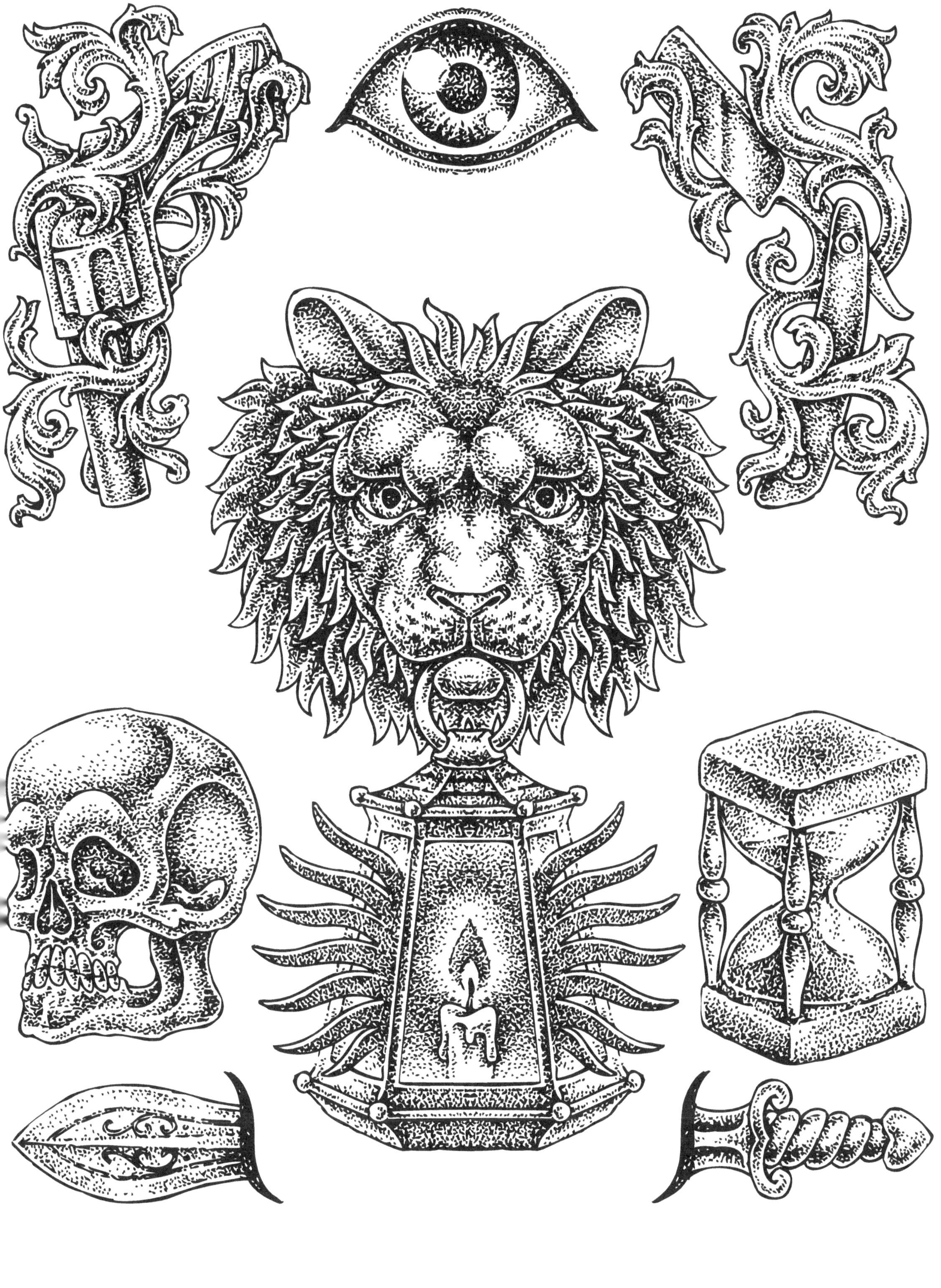

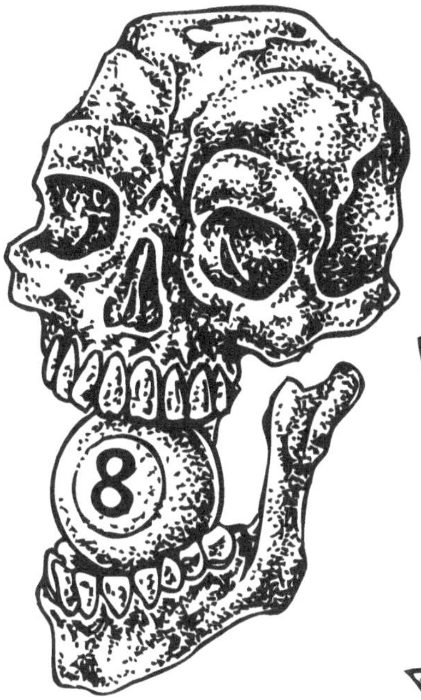
8
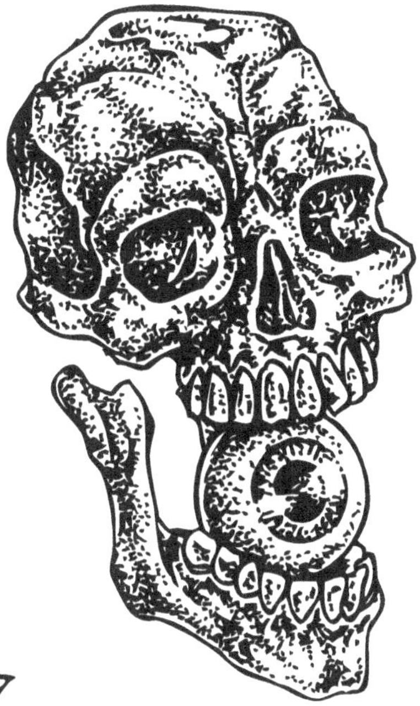
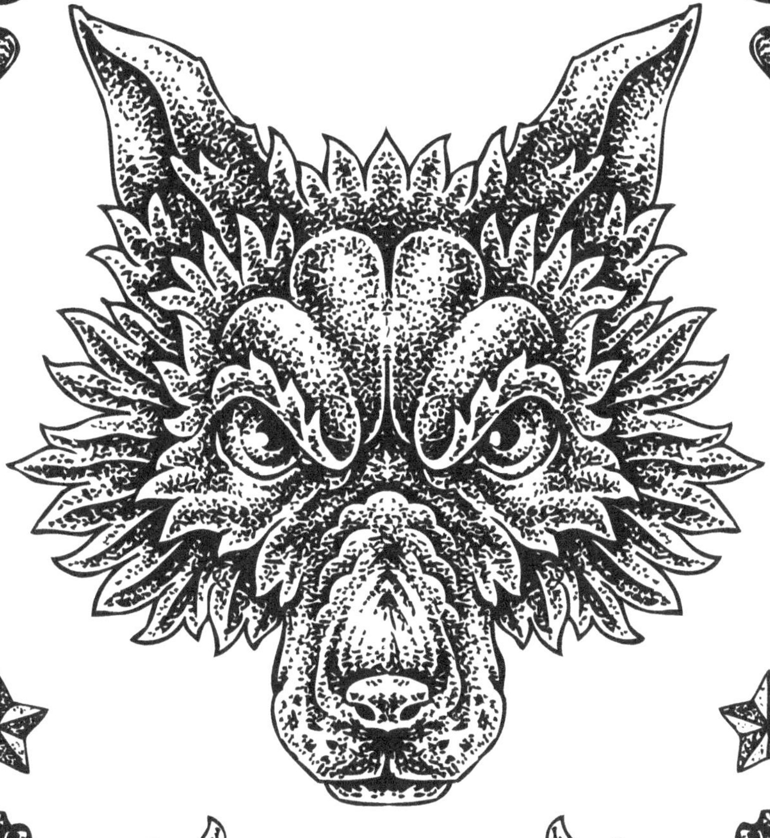
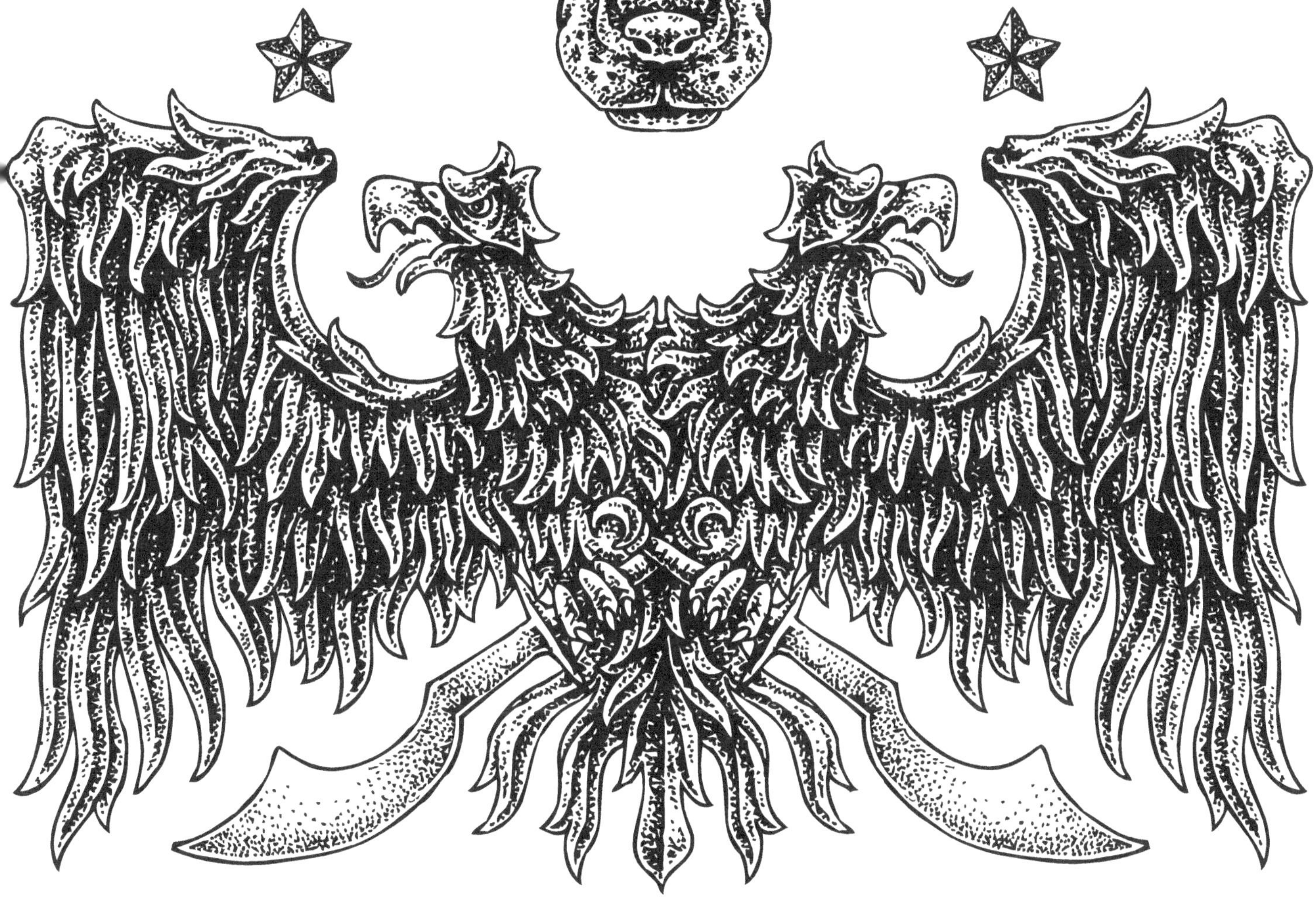

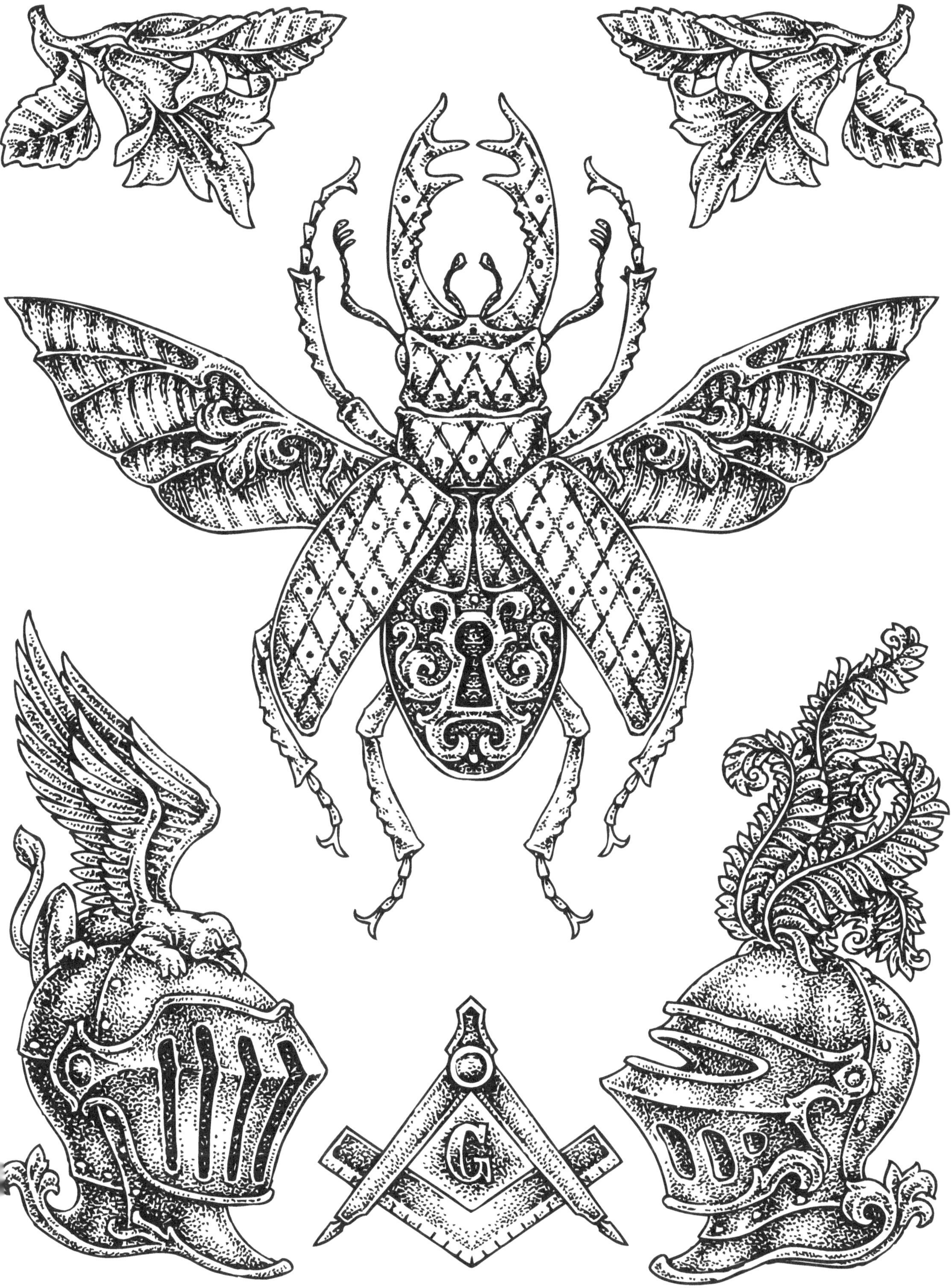
G

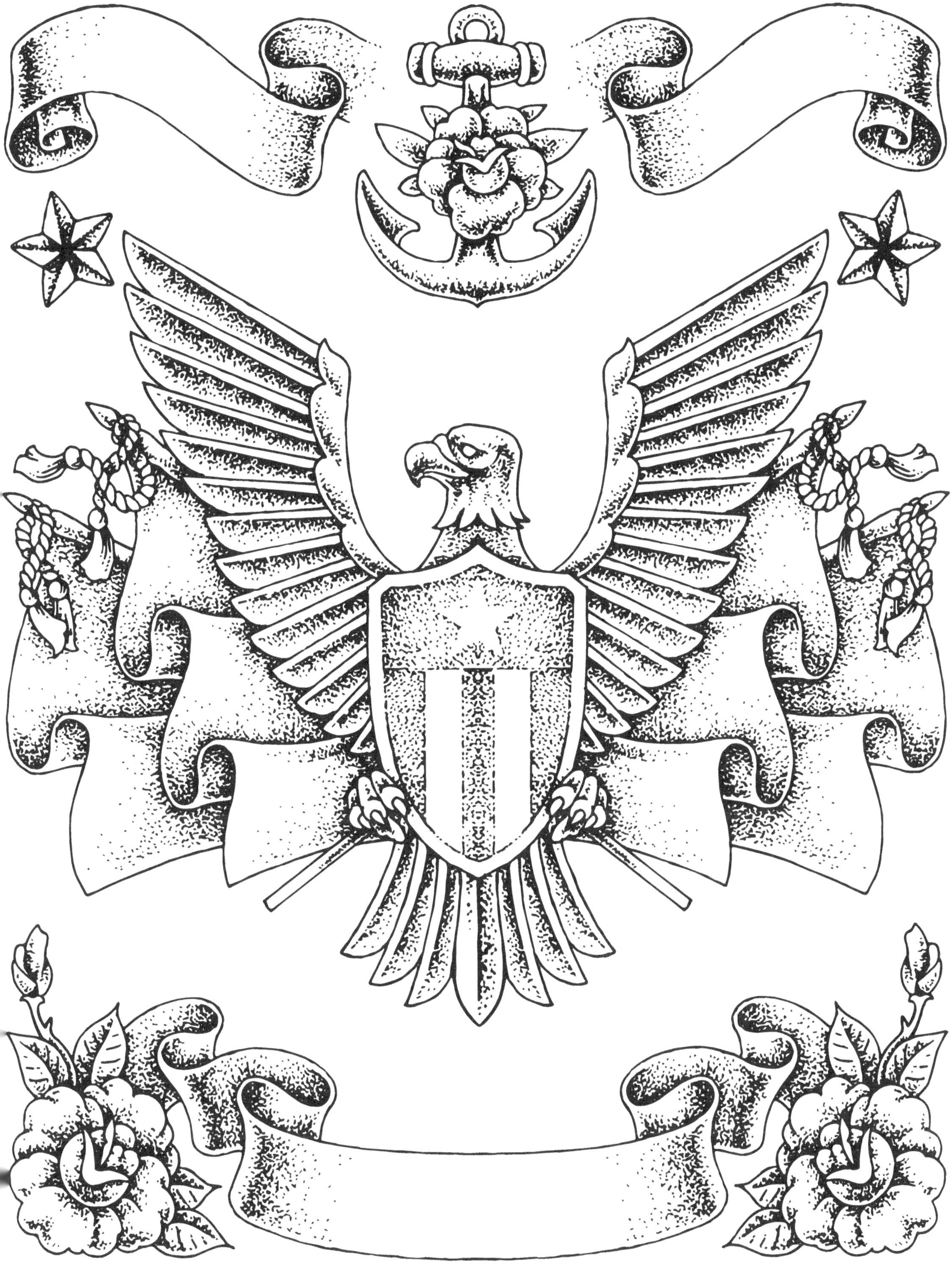

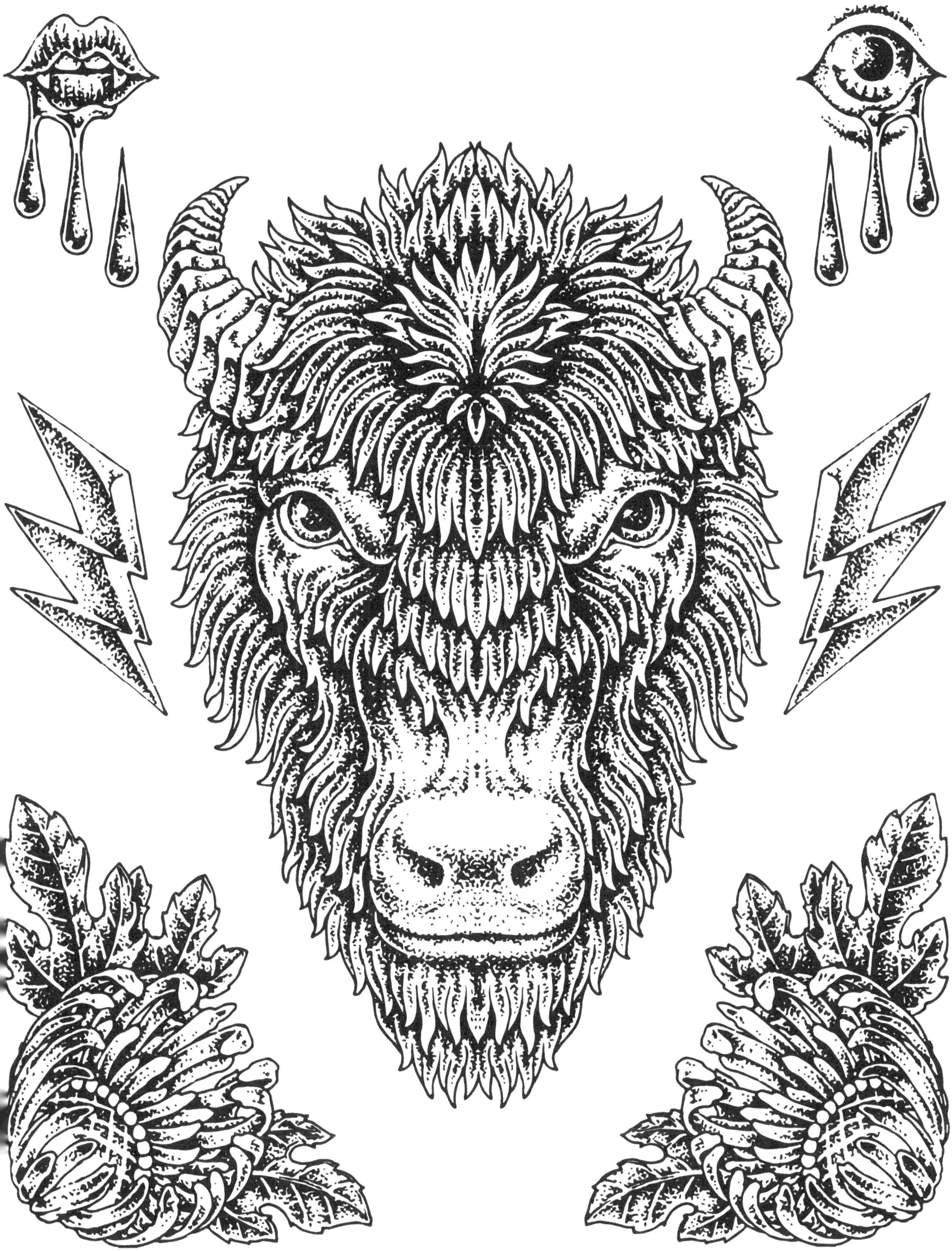

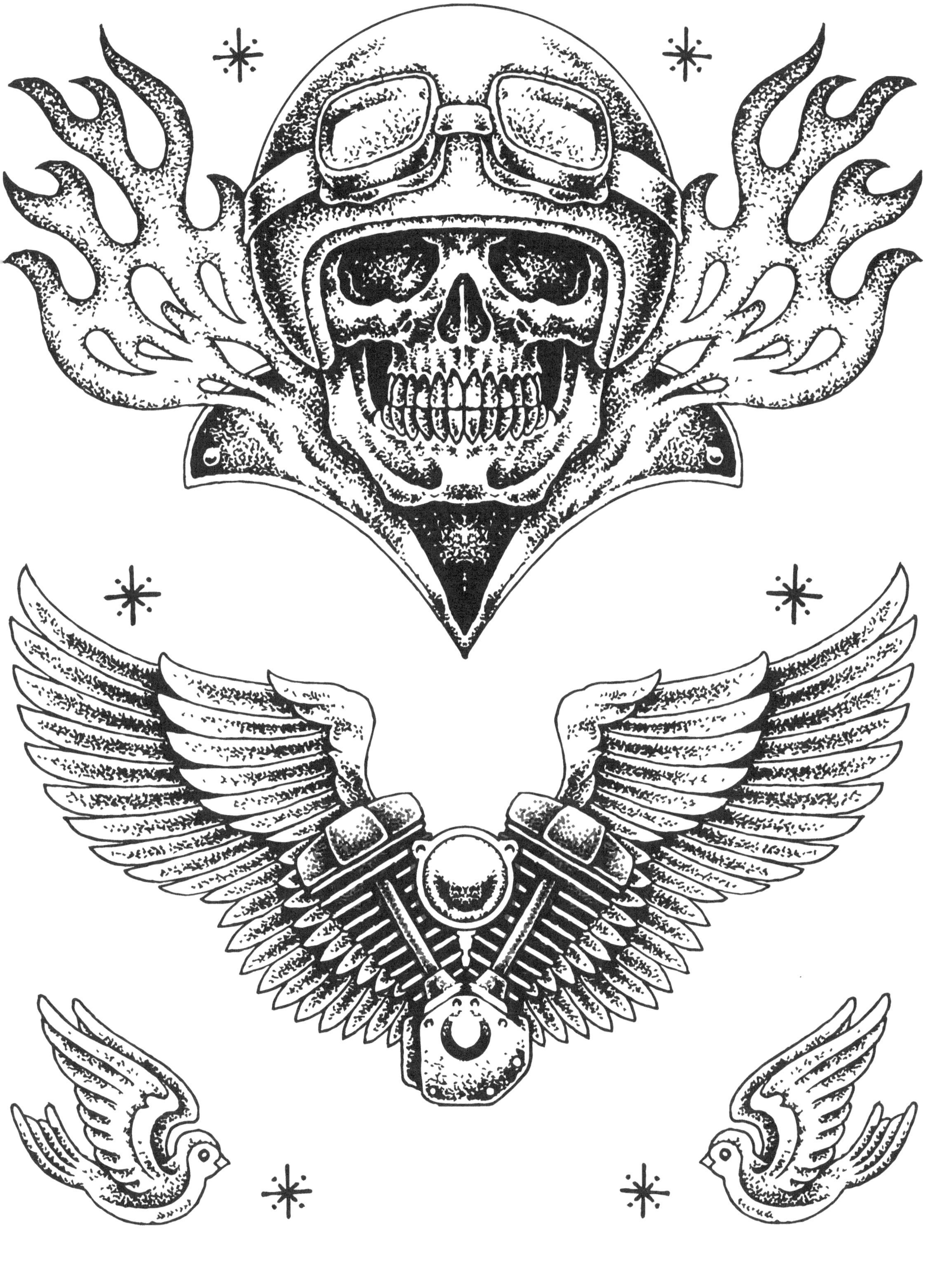

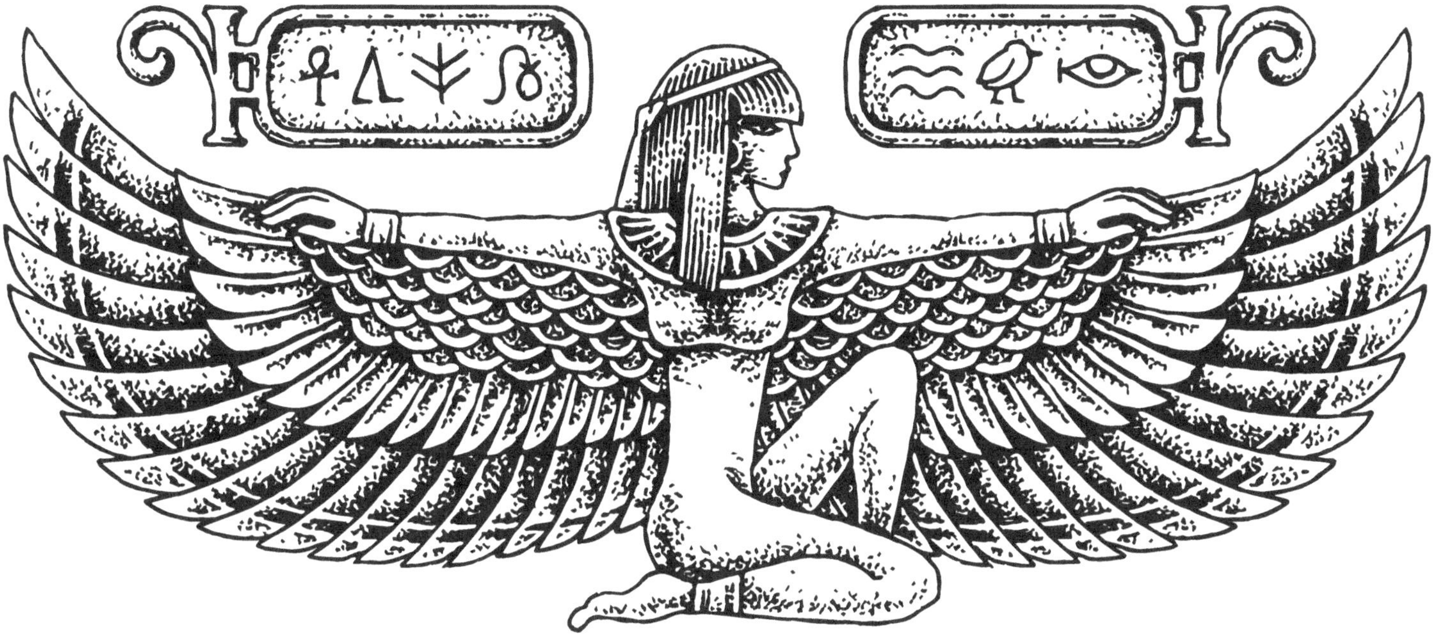

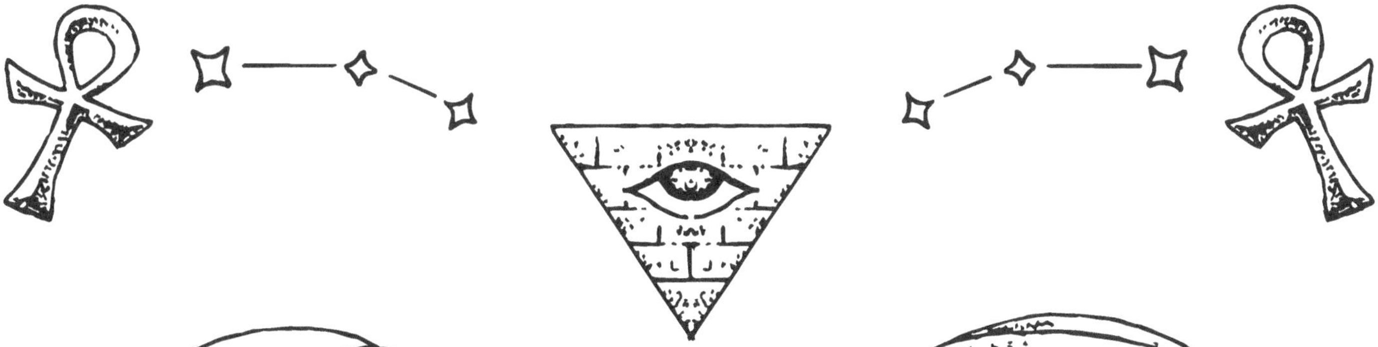

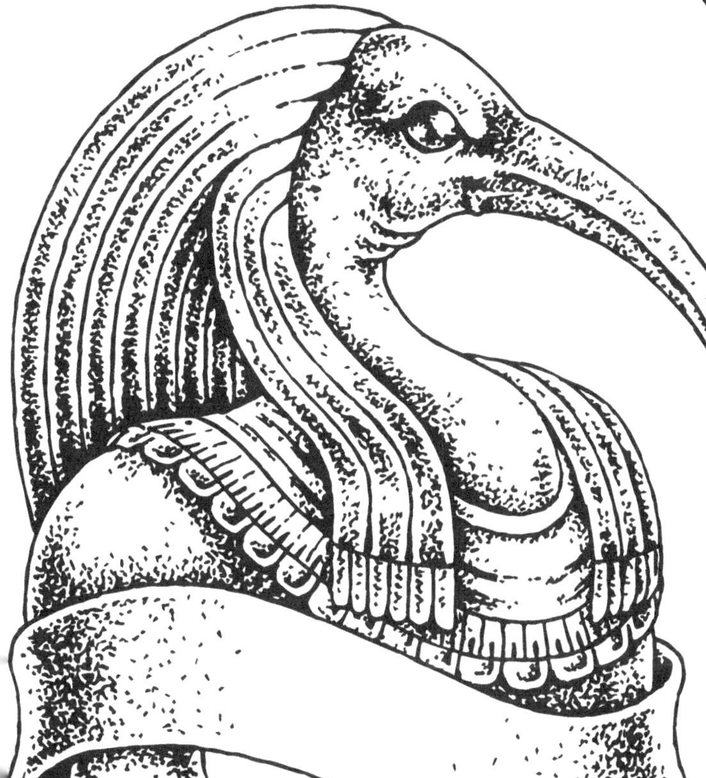

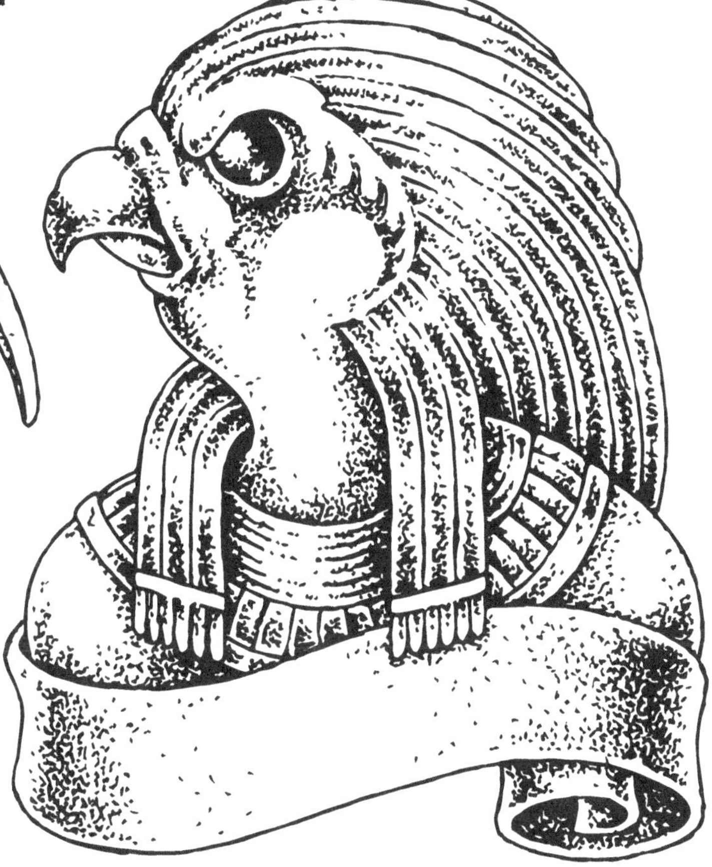

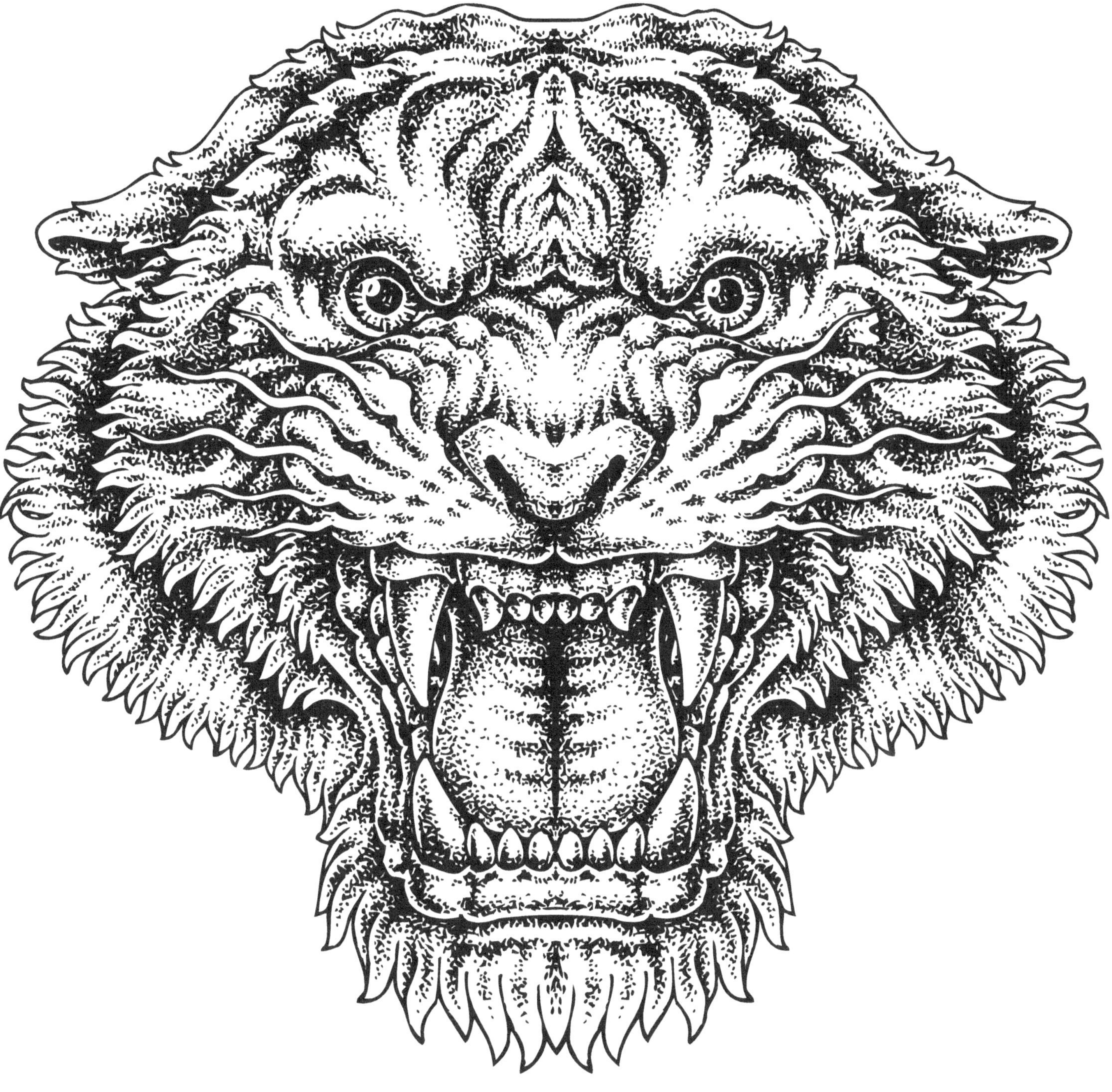

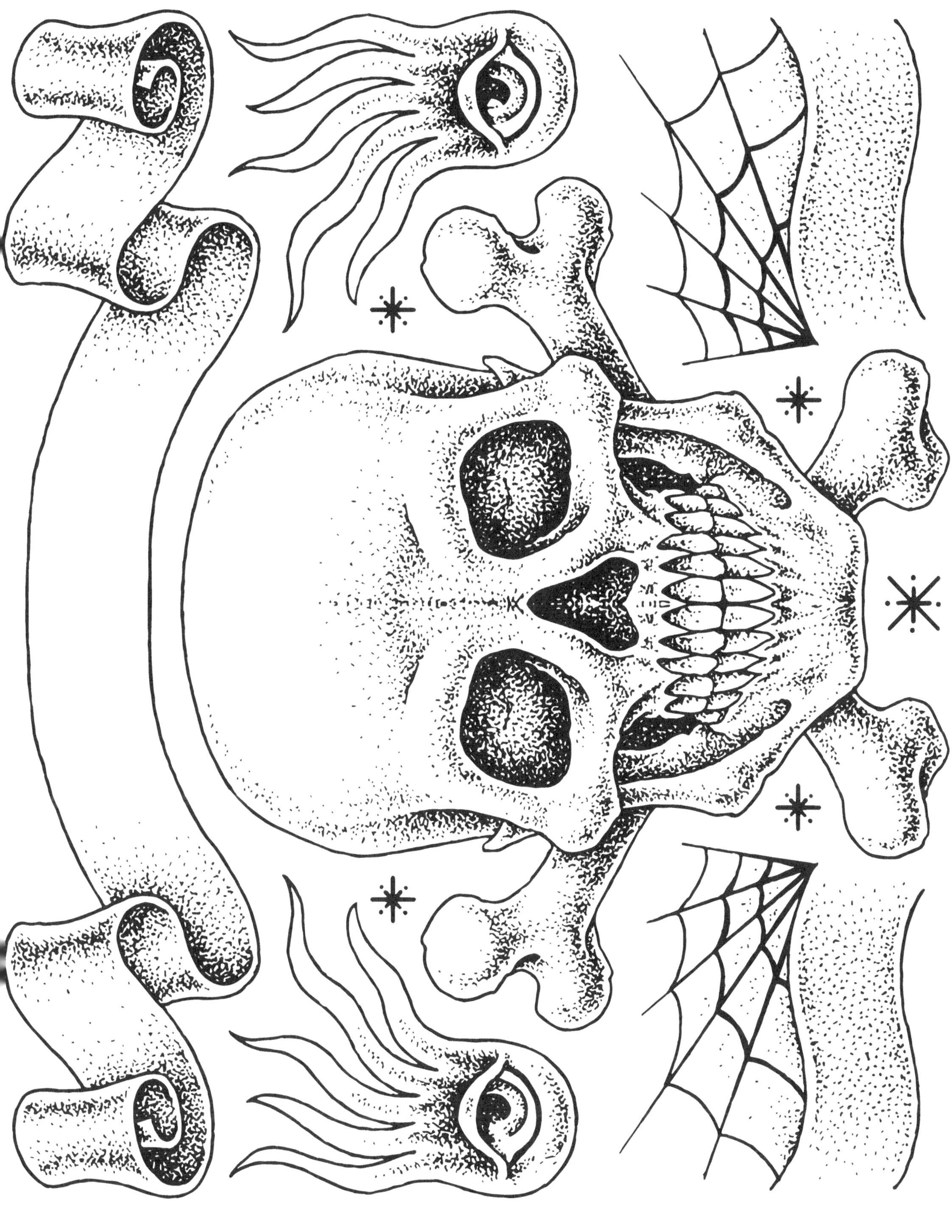

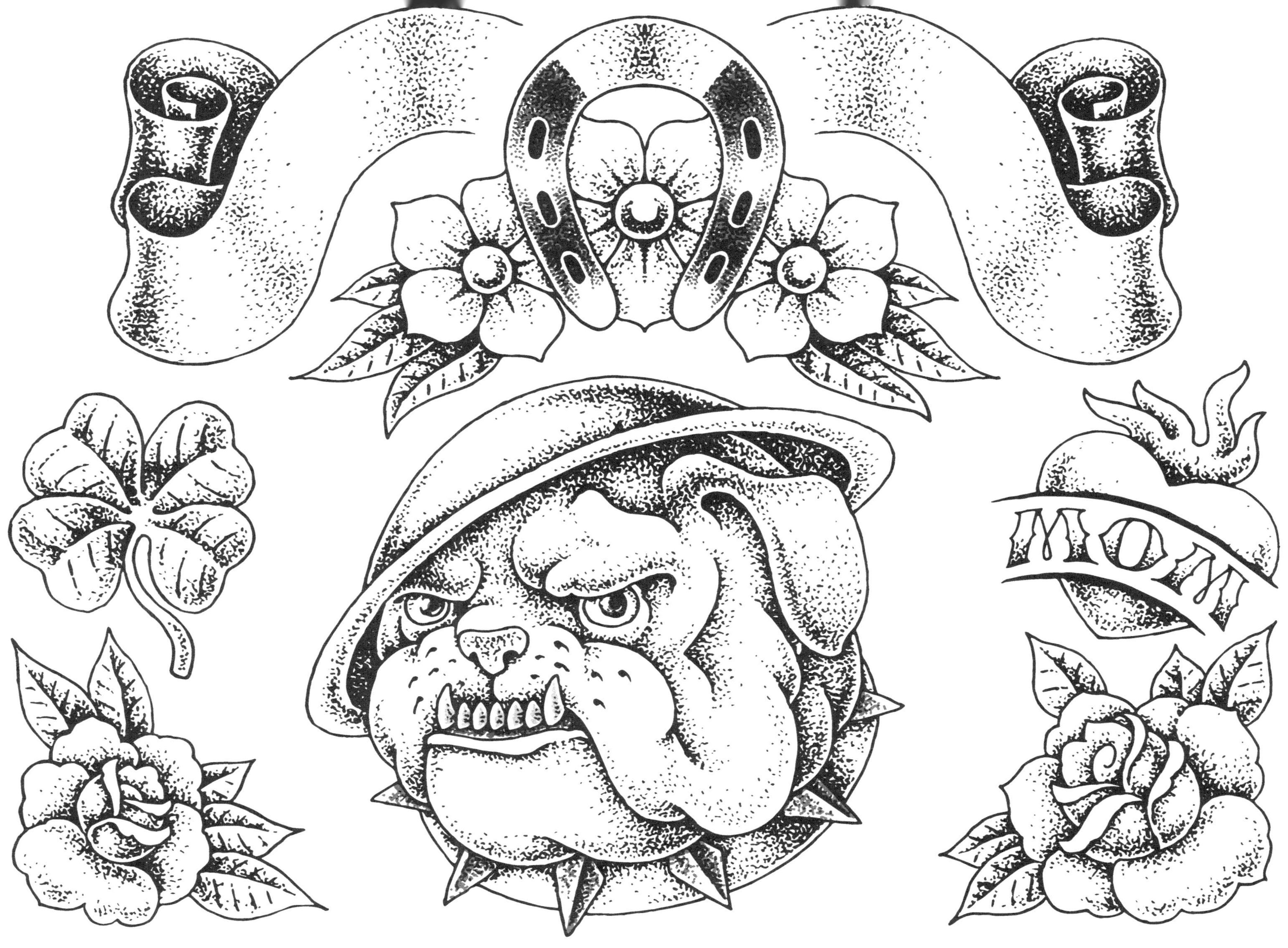
MOM

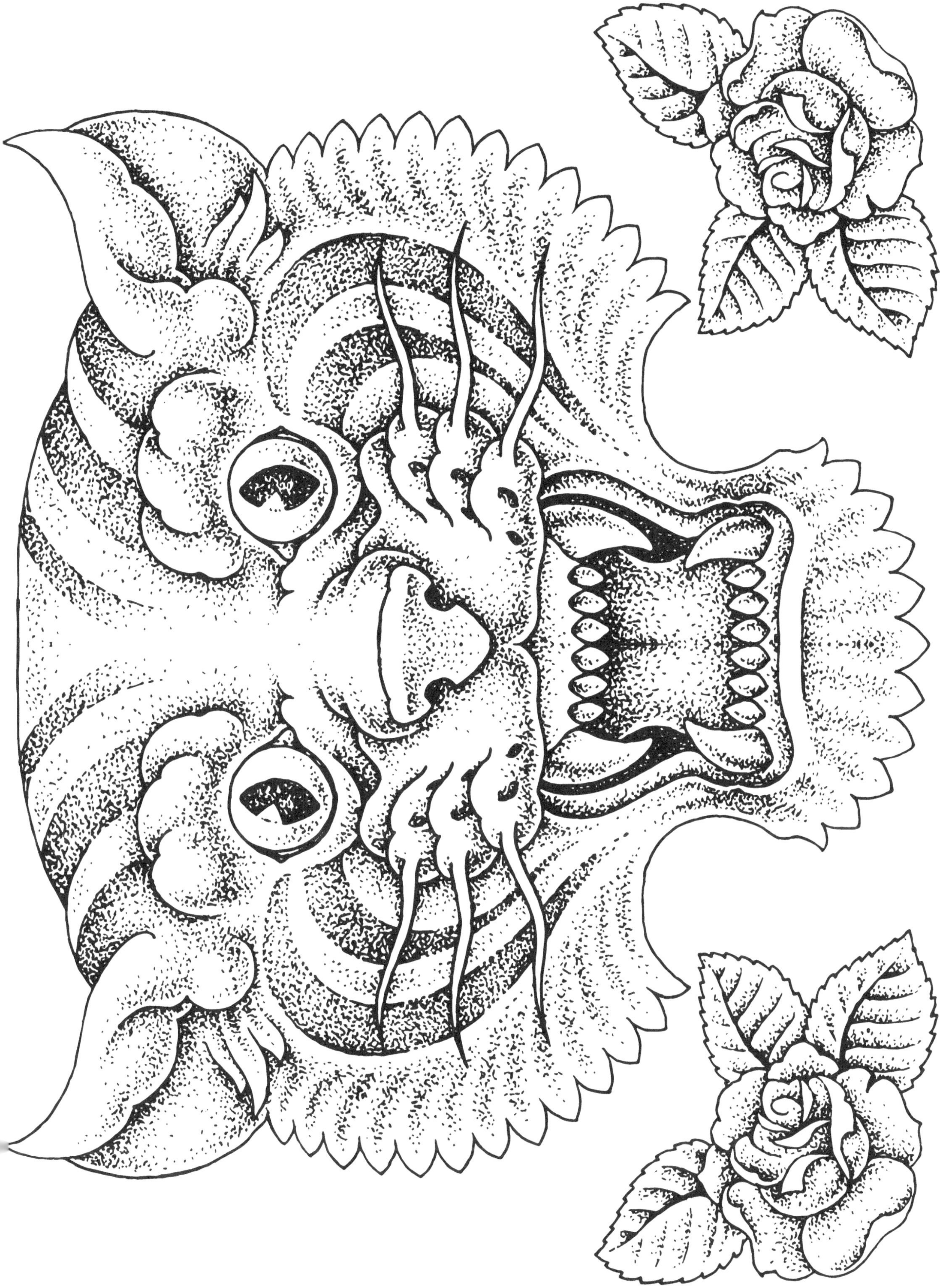

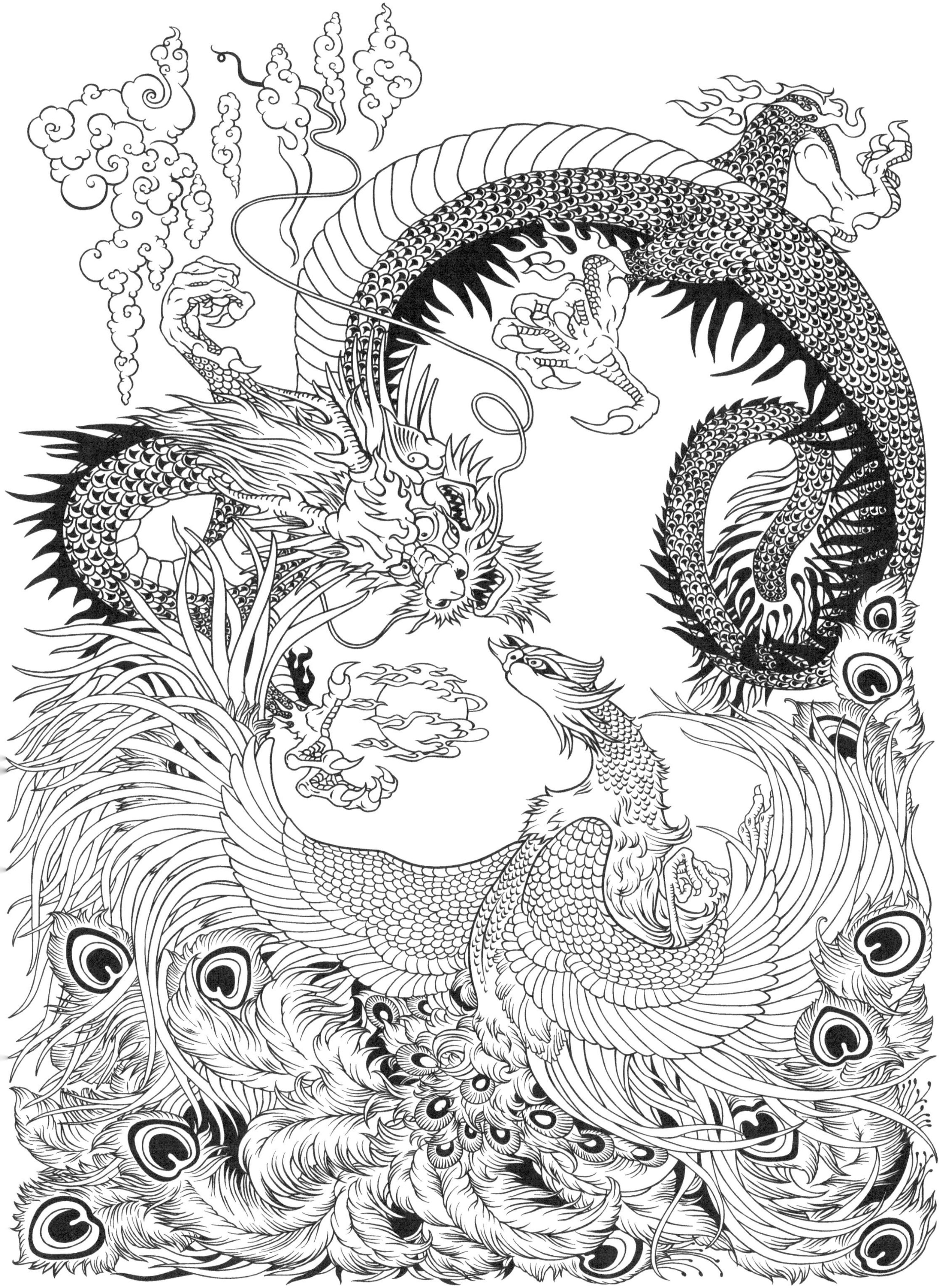

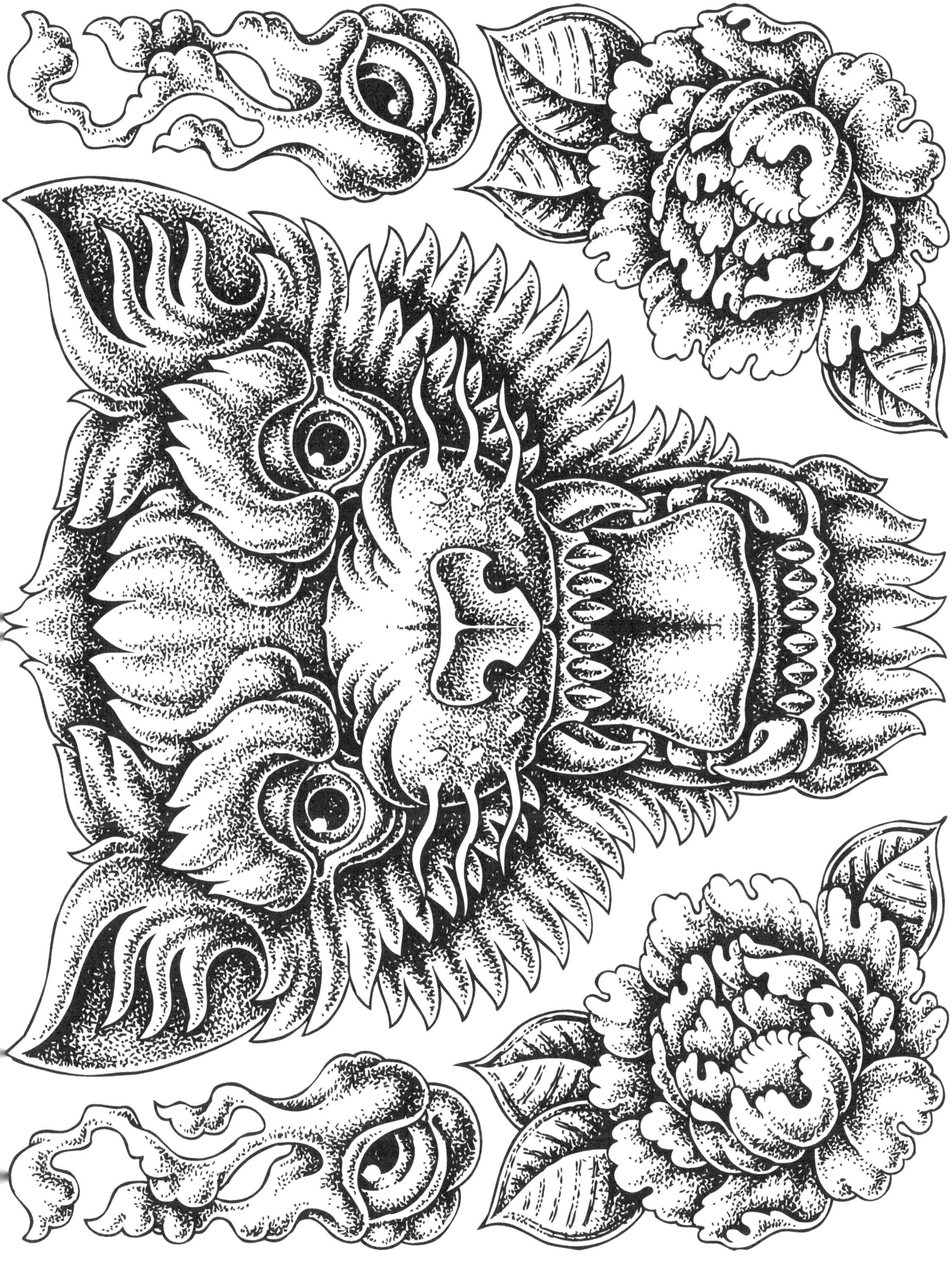

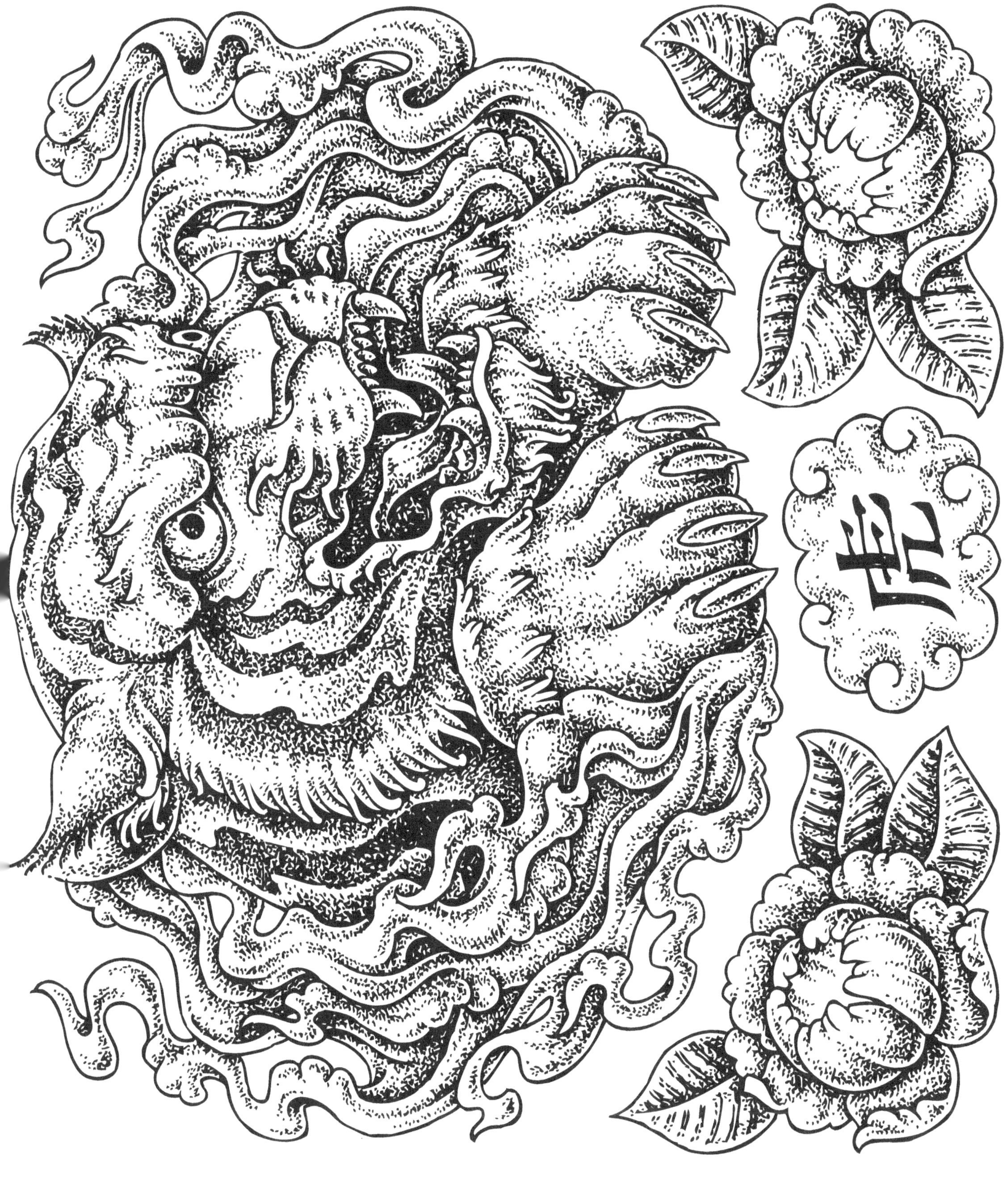

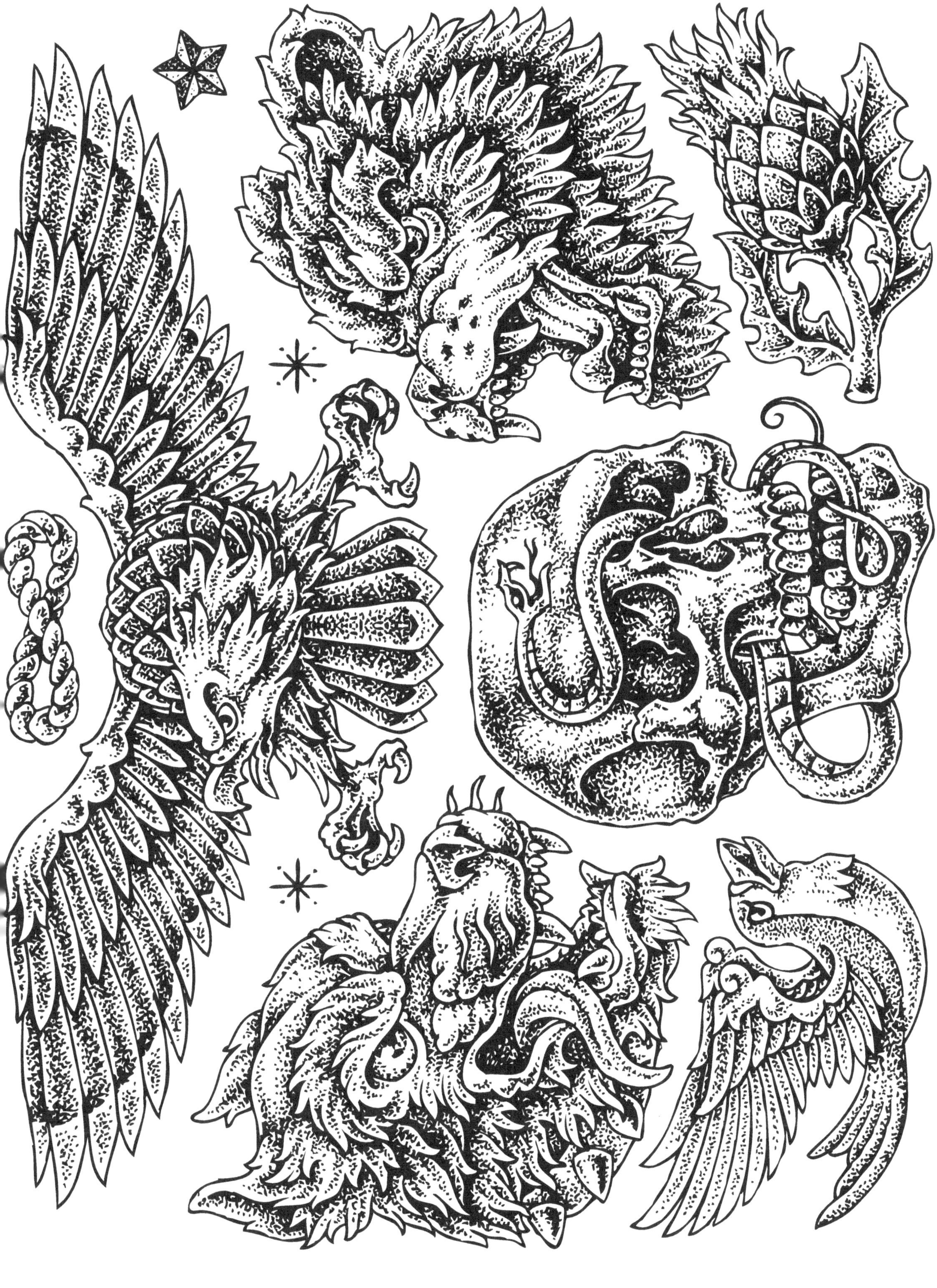

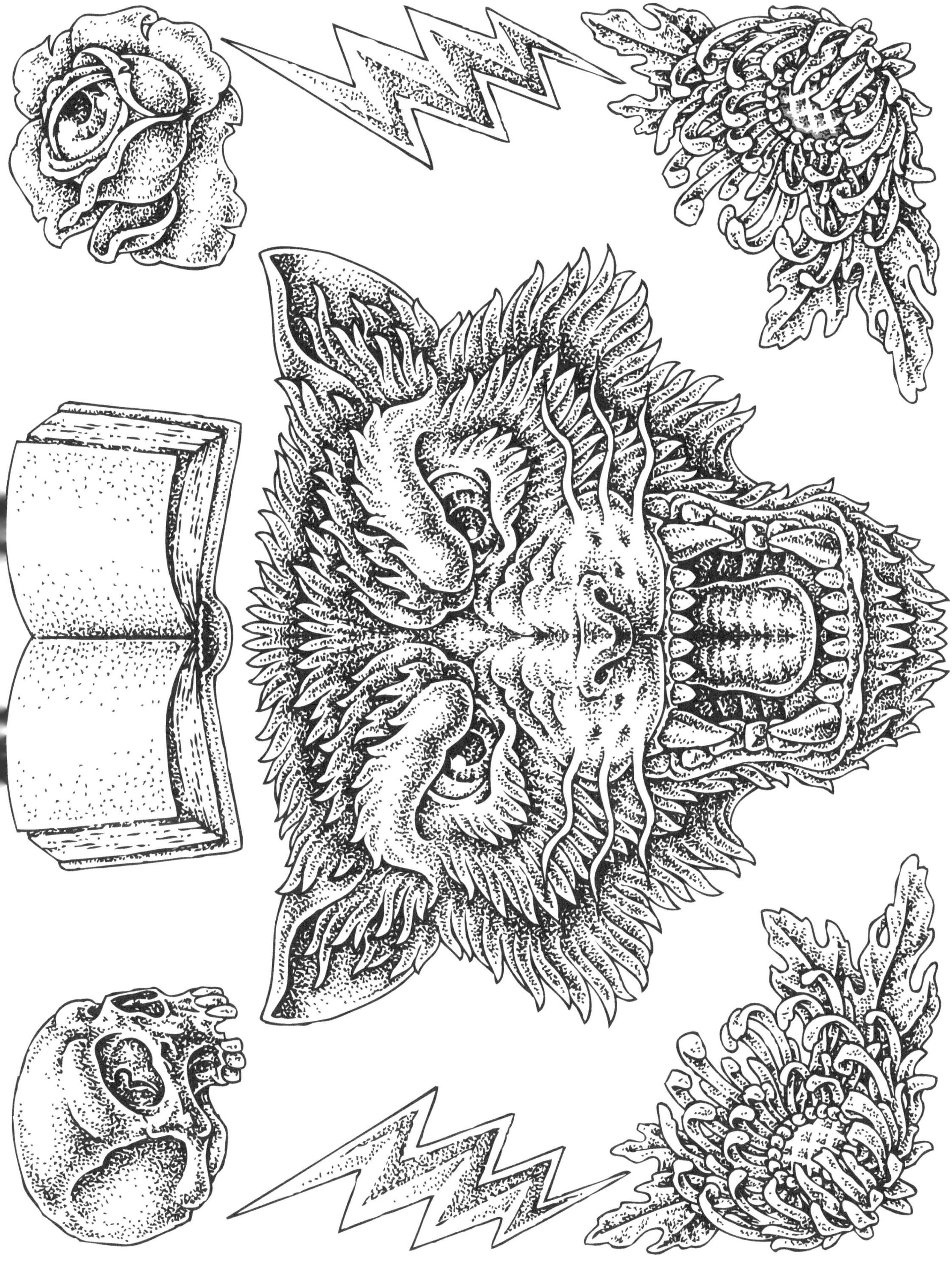

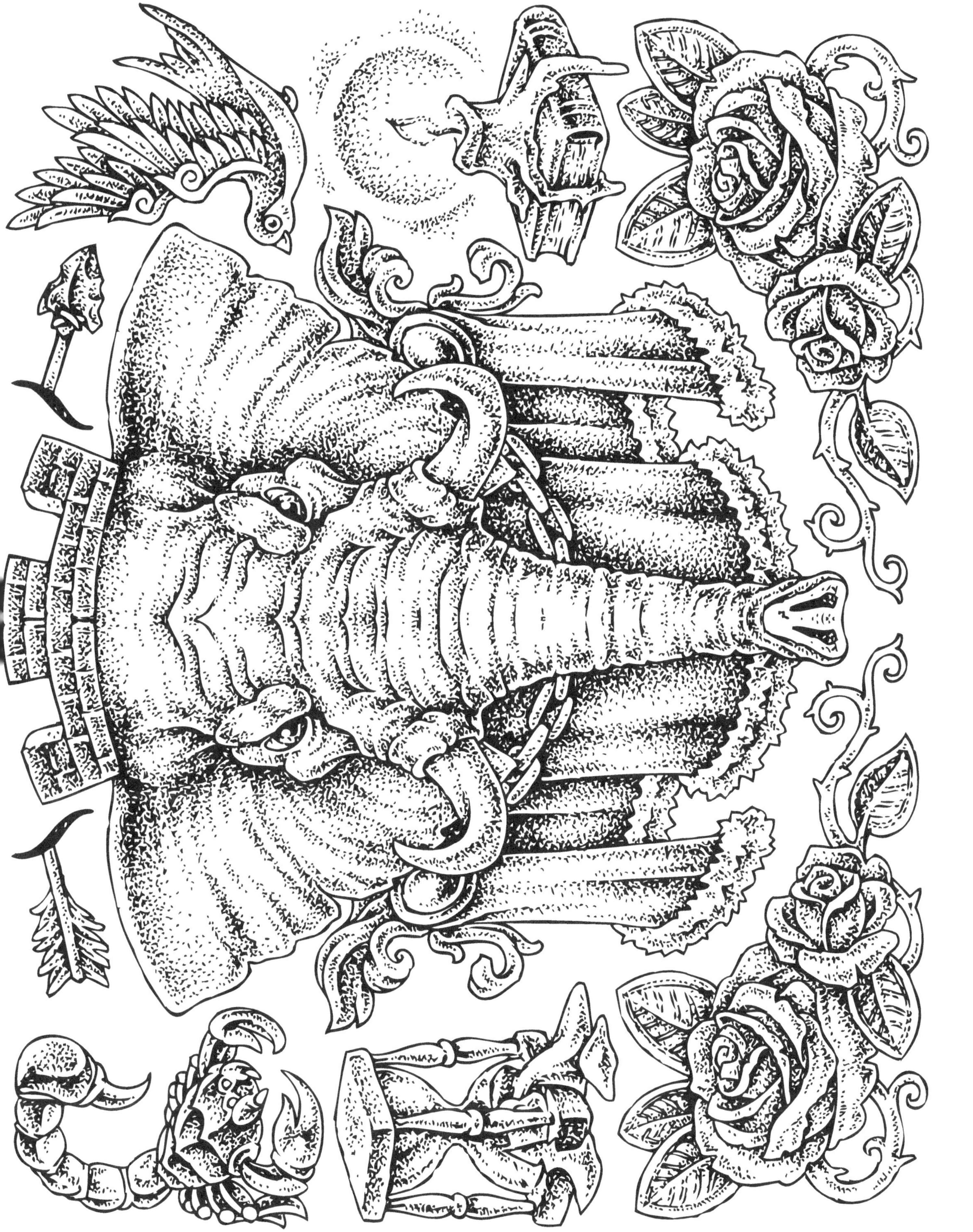

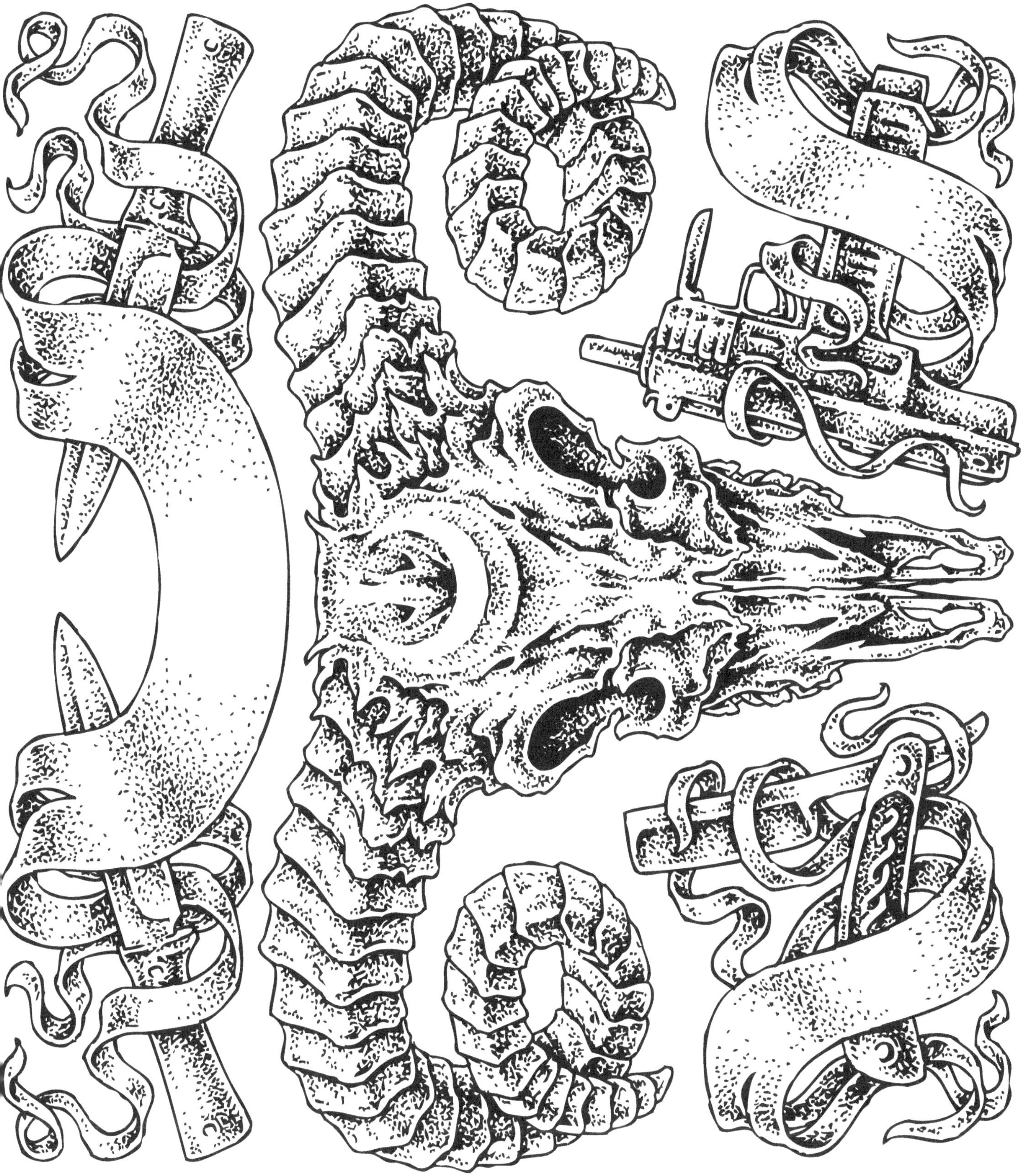

www.ingramcontent.com/pod-product-compliance
Lightning Source LLC
Chambersburg PA
CBHW082254220526
45469CB00009B/2995
* 9 7 8 1 7 2 7 2 7 3 8 6 1 *